INDO DUTCH
KITCHEN SECRETS

STORIES & FAVORITE FAMILY RECIPES
FROM STROOPWAFEL TO RIJSTTAFEL

Jeff Keasberry

INDO DUTCH
KITCHEN SECRETS

STORIES & FAVORITE FAMILY RECIPES
FROM STROOPWAFEL TO RIJSTTAFEL

Jeff Keasberry

www.mascotbooks.com

Indo Dutch Kitchen Secrets:
Stories & Favorite Family Recipes From Stroopwafel to Rijsttafel

1st edition December 2016
2nd edition April 2017

Text, Styling and Photography: Jeff Keasberry
Additional photo source list on page: 246
Design by: Jeff Keasberry

For more information, please contact:
Mascot Books
560 Herndon Parkway #120
Herndon, VA 20170
info@mascotbooks.com

Library of Congress Control Number: 2017904670

CPSIA Code: PRJOS0920C
ISBN-13: 978-1-63177-880-3

Printed in the United States

Sign up for the newsletter, go to **www.keasberry.com**
www.facebook.com/cookingwithkeasberry
www.facebook.com/indodutchcookbook

To my parents and grandparents,
who aroused my curiosity, helped me to develop my taste and
taught me that you can express affection with food.
And to my readers,
that you may come to love Indo Dutch
food through the recipes and stories I have shared.

CONTENTS

No matter where we go, we will always carry with us the aromas that drifted through our house and even welcomed us from outside, to draw us in from the street. It's like a comforting embrace that we hunger for and attempt to hold on to. Could everything we grew up with be magically recreated? Can we relive that savory saltiness, subtle sweetness and refreshing tartness, which is revealed in a variety of fares containing a myriad of exotic spices, specially blended together? The delicacies ranging from mildly seasoned to outright fiery are evoking memories of those we shared it with. We cherish family recipes, passed on not to be lost or gradually forgotten. Who does not remember the flavors and scents of sautéed onions, garlic and shrimp paste? We often find ourselves salivating for those mysterious specialties, prepared with enchanting perfection and pure love…

OMA, JEFF & SPANISH GIRLFRIENDS IN BARCELONA, 1970.

Born above the once-famous restaurant Djokja of my late Oma (Granny) Keasberry, also a well-known cookbook author, I grew up in the family business in Amsterdam, among people whose happiness seemed to largely revolve around food. Eating was at the center of a life full of stories and amusing anecdotes about old times. This is a time that I've never experienced elsewhere, except through the emotional memory of my family. They were the good old days in the tropics, in the former Dutch East Indies - Tempo Doeloe!

Entertaining guests and being a hospitable host is in my blood. Where a *Dutch* family would talk about the weather, our family discussed food. Instead of 'How are you?' the first question asked was: "Have you eaten?" A recognizable Indo Dutch trademark. Whether you were invited or just dropped by, you were always welcome to join us for a meal. As irresistible aromas emanated from the kitchen, you were instructed: "Go to the kitchen and grab a plate!" or, "Pull up a chair!" It's like saying: "Relax and feel at home!"

Indo Dutch food is comfort food, traditionally prepared and recognizable. It contains a sentimental element, which is linked to people, to an experience of Indo Dutch culture. Cooking a meaningful recipe is an emotional experience. It involves feelings of nostalgia, a longing for the past and a desire to want to return to a comfortable home or homeland. It's a cozy visit with mother and father, old friends, departed relatives, a way to connect with your past at the dinner table.

The experience with Indo Dutch food starts with the perception of the exotic scents. Smell is the most evocative of the senses. Every time you smell a familiar dish cooking, that fine memory is recalled. To me, for example, it is the smell of mother's *frikadel pan* (meatloaf), my granny's *ajam smoor* (braised chicken) or my father's *nasi goreng* (fried rice).

I started working at the family restaurant at age 14, and worked my way up to becoming a professional host. Along the way, I learned from my father and mother—and eventually became the third-generation owner of the restaurant at age 18 in 1986. While managing the family business, I completed my formal training at the Hotel & Restaurant Management School in Amsterdam.

As I got older, my interest in my Indo Dutch roots and appreciation for traditions and customs grew. It's what makes us unique and gives us an identity. I felt a need to preserve and pass down the food culture that brought me so much joy.

Carrying on my grandmother's legacy, I authored two cookbooks published in the Netherlands (*Indische Keukengeheimen*, 2012 & *De Nieuwe Indische Keuken* van Jeff Keasberry, 2014)

Both books have been well received by the Dutch press and I have appeared on Dutch national television and radio. My family was featured in an exhibit on the history of the Dutch Indies cuisine at the Tong Tong Fair (the largest Eurasian Festival in the world) for three consecutive years from 2011 through 2013. In my books I explain my perspective on Indo Dutch cuisine. My formative years in a family of restaurateurs and my heritage research makes me uniquely qualified to reveal these international culinary secrets.

"You will be surprised what you can make with just a few ingredients."

Since my move to Los Angeles in 2005, I started craving my mother's cooking, the food that brings me comfort and joy. I learned that little is known about the cultures I belong to and the food that I grew up with. The older Indo Dutch generation in America is slowly fading away and with them, the knowledge on our culinary heritage. There are no relevant cookbooks available in the English language. My passion to pursue the taste of home turned into a mission; I want people to explore and rediscover this unique cooking style, and for it to get the accolades it so richly deserves!

Indo Dutch Kitchen Secrets takes you on a journey of the Indo Dutch diaspora that started in the former Dutch East Indies. It follows the path of the people who traversed different continents and multiple cultures while managing to preserve their heritage to reinforce their identity. It's about a little known secret in the culinary world, a cherished cultural treasure, which is at the heart of this community. It explores and celebrates Indonesian, Dutch and the blending of both in the resultant Indo Dutch fusion cooking style, all coming together in one fascinating cuisine – more than 350 years in the making.

These cuisines are still relatively unknown in the USA. Despite Indonesia being the 4th most populated country in the world (more than 6,000 populated islands), few Americans are familiar with the rich Indonesian and the Indo Dutch fusion cuisine. Indonesian food and Indo Dutch fusion is poised to make an impact in the novelty-hungry culinary world. It can be favorably compared to Thai food and therefore has great crossover potential. There is a growing interest in family recipes, apropos of cultural heritage and traditional cooking styles. The stroopwafel has gone mainstream and now it's time for the rijsttafel and all those other culinary treats to find their way to your table. This cookbook serves to make this all accessible to you.

WHAT IS IN THE COOKBOOK?

- Ingredients and tastemakers explained
- Tips on sourcing ingredients, including substitutes to make things easier
- Special glossary to help you find that special ingredient
- Inspiring ideas for menus and what drinks to serve

Indo Dutch Kitchen Secrets is more than a cookbook. This book also pays homage to the cooks who contributed to the evolution of this cuisine: mothers, grandmothers, fathers and grandfathers included. It's about connecting people, a sense of belonging and joyful togetherness, or as they say in Dutch: *'gezelligheid!'*

"...start your own traditions and create new memories with family and friends."

If you really want a great Indo Dutch meal, you have to go to somebody's house, where you will experience great food. That's why you often found me in my mom's, or granny's kitchen where I learned old school cooking.

Writing this book has been a labor of love and was designed not to just look good on a coffee table, I want you to actually use it and for your guest to say: "This food is delicious!" One of the things I emphasize in this book is going back to basics and enjoying the simple pleasures. The focus is on making this cuisine accessible.

Changing lifestyles also demand for quick-to-prepare and healthy meals. You will be surprised what you can make with just a few ingredients. Whether you are a novice or experienced cook, you can now prepare authentic dishes. Start with the easy recipes and work your way up to more advanced recipes; this way they will appear less intimidating. Having said that, this is not a book on how to cook a meal in 5 minutes. Some dishes do take some time and you may want to get yourself a drink, do some yoga, walk the dog or serve your guests some appetizers while the dish is simmering on the stove. You can also avoid those recipes altogether – there are plenty to choose from.

I hope you really enjoy these dishes. The way my family cooks is not the only way, of course, but it's the way three generations of Keasberry family entertained for more than 50 years. I am happy to share these recipes with you to start your own traditions and create new memories with family and friends.

As I always say: "Gezelligheid begins in the kitchen!" and don't forget to bring this book.

— *Jeff*

PS: These recipes serve as a foundation and inspiration. Apply common sense in the kitchen. Developing your skill to combine and improvise will be more helpful than following a recipe precisely. If you think something you're cooking is missing salt, go ahead and add more! For more tips on cooking and sourcing ingredients, go to page 55.

INDO DUTCH HERITAGE

THE KEASBERRY FAMILY & THE DUTCH EAST INDIES

They say that if you are interested in your family's ethnic heritage, food is one of the best places to start, because it is often the last vestige of cultural traditions to disappear. This book contains my personal memories and anecdotes from family and friends in Holland, Indonesia and the USA, tied to 3 generations' worth of recipes for dishes once served in our family's restaurant which, until today, are still being enjoyed on three continents. It's a celebration of our unique culture and cuisine. This book is intended to connect our past with the here and now, in order to make it relevant and serve as an inspiration for present generations and many generations to come.

I come from a family of strong women. Both my mom and grandmother were entrepreneurs. When we talk about 'fine dining restaurants' and Michelin stars, we usually see male-dominated kitchens, as opposed to my family and the Indo Dutch culture in general, where we see that mostly women rule the kitchen. They spearheaded the evolution and the refinement of Indo Dutch cuisine – they know the traditions and understand the art of cooking. It's fascinating to see a similar matriarchal dynamic in Italian culinary culture. Go to the better restaurants in Italy and you see mostly Italian grandmas being in charge. It is that matriarchal atmosphere and worship that makes Indo Dutch cuisine very personal and homey.

In my book, when I refer to people, culture and cuisine, I prefer to use the term 'Indo Dutch' (other terms used are Dutch Indonesian, Indo European, Indo, Dutch Indies and Indisch), Please, see a more detailed explanation of the different terms on page 239.

There is an abundance of reading material in the Dutch language on the more than 350 years of colonial history in the Dutch East Indies and the emergence of a population with its own specific culture. For my research, I have focused on significant family details, and linked them to historical milestones. Who was where, and what did they do at that time? The Keasberrys originated in England; several descendants eventually settled in the region east of the Indus River, and hence the association with "Indisch" (Dutch Indies) was born. Dutch Indies refers to the former Dutch colony in Southeast Asia (not India), or is frequently seen as a political concept and geographical indication of the area under Dutch control (now Indonesia). Socio-culturally, it refers to the blended culture (subculture) that arose there from European colonialists and their Southeast Asian wives and their multiracial descendants. These people are referred to as Indo-European or Indo Dutch.

The history of the Dutch Indies (from Netherlands East Indies) began with Cornelis de Houtman in 1596, whose merchant fleet dropped anchor in the harbor of Bantam (off the shore of Java). The Portuguese and Spanish merchants had already preceded him. The "Vereenigde Oostindische Compagnie" (Dutch East India Company), or VOC, was established in 1602, thanks to the lucrative trade with the original Spice Islands (the Maluku Islands) in spices such as pepper, cinnamon, mace, nutmeg and cloves. Since no women accompanied the first colonizers, many European men lived with and married indigenous Asian women, who, as of the 19th century, formally belonged to the European population. They were

eventually granted Dutch citizenship, just as their Indo-European progeny, who were raised as European. The children were known as Indo-European, Indo, "Indisch" and also Indo Dutch.

Following Napoleon's conquest of The Netherlands at the end of the 18th century, communication between the VOC and the Dutch in Europe was severed. This led to the isolation of the (Dutch) East Indies, and the VOC disbanded. There was confusion over who had control, and following the British conquest of the islands of Reunion and Île de France, it did not take long before East India also fell under British authority.

Sir Thomas S. Raffles, a British statesman, was named Lieutenant Governor of Java, best known for his founding of Singapore. John Palmer Keasberry Sr., born in 1773 in Bath (near London), was a Lieutenant Colonel during the British self-government (1811-1816). Once Napoleon was defeated at Waterloo (1815), the French occupation of The Netherlands ended; subsequently, the colonial possessions were returned to the Kingdom of The Netherlands. From this time on, the region east of the river Indus became known as The Netherlands East Indies or Dutch East Indies. William Henry Keasberry, born in 1809 in Irichinapaty, Java, son of John Palmer Keasberry Sr. from Bath, England, is the progenitor of all Keasberrys hailing from the Dutch East Indies. His younger brother Benjamin Peach Keasberry established the Presbyterian Church in Singapore in 1843.

Another interesting piece of information is that Keasberry's former house in Singapore was located where the Raffles Hotel now stands. William Henry had a son, Neville Keasberry (born April 24, 1866 in Surabaya and a well-known photographer). One of his sons was my grandfather, Arthur Neville Keasberry (born February 2, 1895 in Surabaya, Netherlands East Indies). In 1921, he married my grandmother Maria Antoinette van Beekom (born 1902 in Gombong, Central Java, daughter of Van Beekom of Zutphen, The Netherlands). This marriage produced six children: Agnes, Cecilia, Donald, Jack, Jim and my father Billy.

In 1942, the Japanese occupation of the Dutch colony began, which continued until 1945. Most Dutch-born Europeans, as well as a great portion of the multiracial population, were imprisoned in internment camps. Grandfather Arthur Neville Keasberry died in 1945. Following Japan's surrender in 1945, the end of the Second World War, the Bersiap Period began: an extremely violent period of lawlessness. During Indonesia's fight for independence, Republican Pemuda (youth) murdered thousands of Indo and Dutch civilians. Due to these political changes Indo life was affected heavily. The Indonesians considered the Indo people to be an extension of colonial power. Suddenly, the Indo and Dutch people became foreigners in their home country. That resulted in a dramatic exodus of all those with Dutch nationality.

When Indonesia became independent after the transfer of sovereignty in 1949, most of the "pure Dutch" and the Indo people of Dutch,

(L TO R) BACK ROW: BILLY, CECILIA (ADJE), DONALD, NESSY, PETER, FRONT ROW: JACK, LIEKE (OMA), JIMMY

British, French, Spanish, Portuguese and German descents were uprooted and many of them decided to repatriate to The Netherlands as Dutch citizens. Some chose New Guinea, but the conditions were bad. Because of the "color bar" some countries like Australia had in place, they only allowed immigrants with European customs and appearance. Only the United States was an exception. In 1949, the government of Indonesia gave the Indo Dutch two years to decide whether to choose Indonesian citizenship (*Warga Negara*). Just a limited number of people opted for this, and in due course, many of those eventually changed their minds and opted for migration to The Netherlands ("spijtoptanten", or those who regretted not choosing repatriation). Ultimately, almost 300,000 Dutch Indies people came to The Netherlands between 1946 and 1964.

Oma (Granny) Keasberry-van Beekom sold her house and fashion boutique 'Maison Keasberry' in Batavia (present-day Jakarta) in 1949, and moved with her sons to The Netherlands as a single parent. With the 1958 created Pastore-Walter Act (PWA) more than 50,000 Indo Dutch people were allowed to immigrate to the United States. Many moved to Michigan, New York, New Jersey, Illinois and Washington. The majority of the Indos can be found in California. Three of Oma's children immigrated to the United States and resettled in California. My mom and dad immigrated in the early 1960s and settled in Los Angeles to build a new future. Oma was left to manage her restaurant but needed support badly. My parents responded to her cry for help and decided to return to Amsterdam to come to the rescue. Shortly afterwards I was born.

Oma Keasberry

My late Oma Keasberry, matriarch and owner of the once-famous restaurant Djokja, was a household name in the culinary world of Amsterdam and the first to popularize Indo Dutch food in the capital of the Netherlands in the early 1950s. Oma Keasberry was author of the best selling cookbook *Oma Keasberry's Indische keukengeheimen* and was considered the authority on authentic Indo Dutch cuisine. To many Amsterdammers, *eating at Oma's* meant visiting Djokja restaurant in the Ferdinand Bolstraat.

"Call me Oma, everyone does! When my restaurant was newly opened, students would often come and help wash dishes to earn a plate of nasi rames. They called me Moesje (Mommy). Now they are doctors, or are climbing the career ladder, and

they still come. Their children have started calling me Oma, this is how I gradually became Oma to everyone."

Oma's full name was Maria Antoinette Keasberry-van Beekom -- her grandchildren called her Oma Lieke and to her nieces and nephews, she was Tante Marie (Aunt Marie). The reputation of the Indo Dutch restaurant, which she owned since 1954, reached far beyond Amsterdam. Not only would some patrons drive for a couple of hours in order to eat at Oma Keasberry's, the restaurant also exported its own home-made sambal to Canada, among other things. Even an entire rijsttafel was special-ordered and flown to Norway via KLM.

Oma Keasberry was born and raised in Gombong in Central Java in 1902. She started a fashion boutique *Maison Keasberry* in the city of Yogyakarta (also known in Dutch as Djokja), and ran it for 25 years. Following the surrender (capitulation) on September 4, 1945, she lost her husband, after which she moved to Weltevreden, Jakarta (known as Batavia at that time). There, she started up another fashion boutique, which she ran until 1949. *"In the time before the war -- when I had a fashion boutique in Djokja -- I worked for numerous people. I mostly worked for the well-to-do. Hence, I worked for the Governor of Djokja, Mrs. Adam, and for a variety of doctors' wives. I also organized fashion shows at the clubhouse and the concours d'elegance. I even participated myself, and once won first place."*

From Maison Keasberry
To Restaurant Djokja

In 1950, Oma moved to The Netherlands with her sons, where she lived on the Stadhouderskade in Amsterdam. She started up a fashion boutique, Maison Keasberry, on the Ferdinand Bolstraat. After working in the fashion boutique for four years, she decided that she preferred cooking after all, and longed to start something for herself.

And so Oma Keasberry established Djokja restaurant in the Ferdinand Bolstraat, named after the city she had lived in for many years. In the beginning, the children often helped out. Oma herself was in the kitchen and did the cooking. Jack worked on the business end and his wife frequently lent a hand as well. Billy and Peter, her son and grandson, also helped. The two boys went out in the cold on their bicycles and delivered the food in a *rantang* (multi-layered food carrier) to customers at home. Very quickly, Djokja became a successful business. Oma had a gift for cooking: "You have to have the knack for it; cooking is an art," she would often say. Oma Keasberry loved cooking. It was simply part of her. She saw it as an exciting challenge to cook with ordinary, inexpensive ingredients, and transform them into a sumptuous meal.

"You have to have the knack for it; cooking is an art."

Throughout the years, her customers would ask for the recipes, so that they too would be able to prepare the things they had enjoyed with such relish at Oma's place. No big surprise, then, when you learn that the former Sultan of Pontianak demanded she prepare his meals whenever he stayed at the Hotel des Indes, as though there were no chefs there. In 1976, Oma published her cookbook *Oma's Indische keukengeheimen* (Oma's Indo Dutch Kitchen Secrets). She autographed many editions at that time, and she would often add the inscription: "It's all in here, but if you really want to know how it tastes, you will have to come eat at Oma's."

You have to have a flair for cooking. The knack, as Oma called it, is a family trait. Her own mother was also a superlative cook, and several of the Keasberry children have inherited the same flair. Of her daughter-in-law Jessy, Oma has said: "It's as though she inherited the same talent from us. She is a wonderful cook. And that's a good thing, too, because although I want to continue doing this work for quite a while longer, there will come a time when I will have to pass some of the responsibilities on to others. So it is good to know that your own family can maintain the reputation of your business to the highest standards."

Oma Keasberry worked at the restaurant twelve hours a day. Most often, she could be found standing at the cash register, where she could oversee everything with a watchful eye. In addition, she always assisted with the preparation of the food: tasting, improving, creating new items, and experimenting. As she advanced in years, Oma occasionally thought about taking things a little easier. After 25 years, Oma handed the restaurant over to her son Bill and daughter-in-law Jessy.

"Oma is always there for the preparation of the food. She tastes, improves, and creates new items. Every week, I learn new things."

— *Jessy*

MAISON *Keasberry* **MAAT-EN CONFECTIEATELIER**

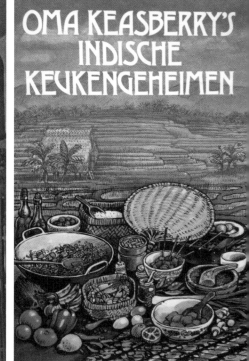

OMA KEASBERRY'S INDISCHE KEUKENGEHEIMEN

INDISCH-EUROPEES RESTAURANT „Djokja"

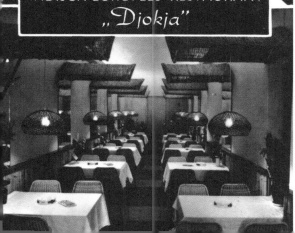

Jessy Chevallier - Keasberry

For more than 26 years, Djokja restaurant was run with the support of my mother, Jessica Chevallier-Keasberry. She started out as a server, then became hostess, executive chef and co-owner. She is my ideal example of patience, trust and tenacity. She is renowned for her creativity and ingenuity in the kitchen. Her refined dishes made even the most finicky gastronome return time after time. She contributed to the first edition of Oma Keasberry's bestselling cookbook and again, has lovingly contributed to this book by passing along many of her recipes and refining Oma's recipes.

My mother was born just before the Second World War in Batavia (now called Jakarta), where her father Jan Chevallier was employed as a customs officer. She is the youngest daughter of four children. At the age of 11, she was sent to the Netherlands by airplane with a sister and a brother. When she was an 18-year-old young woman, she left home and rented rooms in Amsterdam; at one point she decided to get a bite to eat at Djokja. Her cousin Eriana encouraged her to apply for a job. At the time, she was working as a nurse in elderly care, but when Mrs. Keasberry (her future mother-in-law) mentioned that she was looking for a server, my mother could not refuse the opportunity. This is where she met my father, and they began a relationship. After my mother had worked at Djokja for a few years, she decided to take on a new challenge. She emigrated to the United States by herself, where her father (my grandpa) was already living. Some time later, my father followed. Following an urgent cry for help from his mother in Amsterdam, my father

decided to re-join his mother in the restaurant. He returned to Amsterdam with his fiancée, where they subsequently married. From this marriage, two sons were born: my brother Duncan and I.

Seasoning, roasting and baking was in my mother's blood, and in due course, she moved from serving to standing over the pots and pans in the kitchen. It soon became apparent that she had a natural talent. With the touch of a sorceress, she went to work, blending and sampling. As a prominent culinary journalist once recounted: "A culinary exploration with the sweet, bright and lovely Jessica as your guide, your voyage is undoubtedly destined to be an absolute success, where you no longer feel as though you are in the Ferdinand Bolstraat, but somewhere distant on Palembang, Java or Sumatra. The undertones of Jessy's quiet, mighty power can be found in the dishes which change on a daily basis. Time and again, she surprises you with a dish or small bite which you have never tasted before." Together with my father Bill, she took over her mother-in-law's restaurant. In 1984, they changed the name of the restaurant to "Djokja-Baru" ("New Djokja") to herald a new era after the transfer of ownership. Under Jessy's culinary leadership, the catering and party services divisions were expanded, and elaborate buffets were organized for the Hilton Hotel in Amsterdam, among others. In addition, large companies such as Akzo, Adidas and Philips were presented with her specialties. She did not even blink at managing events for 1,500 people. To this day, my mother still makes the most tantalizing dishes.

Bill Keasberry

My father, Billy Neville Keasberry, was the youngest of all of Oma's children. He was born in Djokja, arrived in The Netherlands at the age of six, and grew up in his mother's restaurant. He was considered the "heir to the throne" and as such, was enlisted by his mother to deliver the take-out orders from a very early age.

My father was an enterprising man with an uncommon talent for hospitality and entertaining. He was a *bon vivant*, a gregarious man, who could unabashedly approach people from any social status, and welcome them into his own lively circle of friends. He was very creative, with liberal ideas about business operations, and he did not take kindly to being told what to do. This created some friction between mother and son. Despite his mother's conservative management style, he frequently succeeded in convincing her of his bold plans. The restaurant was renovated and expanded five times under his leadership.

Tante Dee, My Other Oma

Patrons who had not made a reservation for the more elegant, remodeled front room, were immediately ushered to the back room by Oma Keasberry. This was the domain of my other grandma, Dee Delhaye. To regular customers, she was known as Tante Dee (Aunt Dee).

The back room had not been renovated, and still had thatched roofs and wicker chairs. The atmosphere had a tropical feel. This is where I began my career as busboy. I was fourteen years old, and was allowed to clear the tables, wearing my black trousers and white *jas-tutup* (a type of Nehru jacket). If I had done my best, Oma Dee would tuck a small tip into my hand. Oma Dee had arrived in The Netherlands much later, in 1966. Eventually she was offered a job at Djokja restaurant. To us, she was the archetype of never-ending optimism and perseverance. She continued helping out in order to support her children and grandchildren.

INDO DUTCH DIASPORA

Netherlands

After Indonesia became independent, the majority of the Indos had to leave the home country behind to start a new life in the fatherland: the Netherlands.

Indo Dutch people have shown to adapt themselves pretty easily, but this was also a form of self-preservation. Many repatriates from the former Dutch East Indies were housed in so-called *contractpensions* (state-contracted boarding houses). Once you acted fully assimilated, you would be granted independent housing.

During that period civil organizations and government patronized the Indo Dutch, with a narrow-minded conception about that group in the 1950's. The Netherlands equated cultural differences with cultural backwardness. Moreover, the Netherlands wanted to close the chapter of colonial history as fast as possible.

As a result of having to focus on adjusting to society in the Netherlands, many Indo Dutch people suppressed and denied their own cultural background. They were silent about traumatic experiences during the war and the Bersiap period. Due to their own war experiences, people in the Netherlands had no time to listen to "the stories of the Indo Dutch people." When someone showed interest in your background, you would rather keep the good and bad memories about the old times to yourself.

As a result, kids of the first generation Indo Dutch parents were often confronted with the "silence" of their parents, with reference to their "Indisch" past. You would rather not talk about that which makes you vulnerable. The experiences during the wartime, the Japanese occupation and Bersiap period in particular, have made

the situation more complex for the first generation and also for their kids, who were born shortly after that. The combination of cherished memories on the one hand, but also the war traumas on the other, have made remembering the past extra complicated for first and second generations.

The largest group of people with roots in the former Dutch East Indies is in the Netherlands. The highest number of Indonesian restaurants and grocery stores can be found in the Netherlands. Nearly every month a town organizes a Pasar Malam (Indo Dutch themed bazaar), the oldest and largest is the Tong Tong Fair, which is held in The Hague. I call it the Indo Dutch village and it is the largest Eurasian festival in the world. So, in terms of cultural maintenance there are plenty of places to go and things to do.

USA

More than 50,000 Indo Dutch people migrated from the Netherlands to the United States, under the Pastore-Walter Act (PWA – created in 1958).

The Indo Dutch family culture in the USA subscribed to the concept of the "American Dream," and encouraged their children to pursue education as a way of getting ahead in the new society. The best way to do that was to assimilate quickly and speak English at home. As a result, the offspring lost the ability to speak Dutch – an important part of the Indo identity. Therefore, the kids and grandkids of first-generation immigrants consider themselves more American and are a bit more removed from their Indo Dutch roots and culture as the Indo Dutch people in the Netherlands. Part of that Indo identity is being able to understand and speak Dutch… and that was not often done at home. I see it as a parents' responsibility to pass on their

DE SOOS

culture and language. Like René Creutzburg (publisher of *De Indo* magazine) said: "My kids were young when we arrived. In my house we had one rule. The whole day you can speak English and we will even reply in English, because that's now your language. However, the hour we are together at the dinner table, we speak Dutch. Boy, was it quiet at the table! Now they are older they boast to friends that they speak another language, even though not much."

René met Tjalie Robinson (aka Jan Boon, intellectual and writer) in California and he expressed his desire for Indos to begin a society. In June of 1963, De Soos was established - the first Indo Community Center. Once per month Indos would come together, the second of the month in the early afternoon. The objective was to strengthen the community by supporting each other, and for everyone to participate in organized activities for adults and kids. There was a need for new immigrants to share experiences and telephone numbers. De Soos closed its doors after 25 years in 1988.

Out of the most popular Indo Dutch clubs in Southern California: AVENDO, ROSIE, WAPENBROEDERS, AHOI, HOLLAND SOCCER CLUB, NAS and AVIO, only the last 3 are still active. A popular annual event for the Dutch community is the Holland Festival, organized by the United Netherlands Organizations. The first was held in 1988 and started out to be a typical Dutch affair, which has evolved into more of a *pasar malam* style event, popular among Americans with Indo Dutch roots who make up about 70%

of the total visitors. The event has become a popular reunion for friends and family who enjoy each other's company, listening or dancing to Indo Rock and of course enjoying good Indo food.

Tempo Doeloe

For many, the Dutch East Indies remains a mystery. The country they left behind has never left them; it continues to haunt and tempt, with the time spent in Indonesia often viewed in retrospect through rose-tinted glasses. At any Indo Dutch gathering, no matter where in the world, sooner or later the topic of conversation always veers around *Tempo Doeloe* or *the good old days*. This period is originally referred to as the time between 1870 and 1914, when the first World War started and they are also referred to as the living memories of ex-colonials in diaspora. Animated stories of dances, picnics, hunting, house parties and estates in the tropics are recounted with a hint of nostalgia in their voices. A time when life was easy, unspoiled by modern technology and one could afford to hire three or four servants to maintain the household. Sitting around the dinner table and enjoying Indo Dutch comfort food, is a way of coping with the loss of the Dutch Indies, the experience of displacement, violence and retaliation during the process of decolonization and repatriation to the Netherlands.

INDO DUTCH STYLE

What is it that makes the Indo Dutch way of life so different? This is the question that sprang to mind as I stood in the kitchen, whipping up batter for *pandan* cake. There are characteristics that typify *Indies* (Indische) people: whether you are a *Totok* (an Indonesian language term colloquially used in Indonesia to refer to full-blooded individuals of Dutch and other European ancestry who lived in the Dutch East Indies until Indonesian independence), or an *Indo* (short for Indo-European, of mixed race, with roots in the Dutch East Indies. A mix of predominantly Dutch, and also Portuguese, British, French, Belgian, German and others with Javanese, Sumatran, Manadonese, Timorese, Ambonese, Chinese, Balinese, etc. The word Indo-European has been used since the nineteenth century during the height of Dutch colonial rule. The first part, Indo, is derived from the Greek *Indoi,* which means India and in turn is derived from Indus. Indo in this context is not derived from Indonesia; it is a term coined by James Richardson in 1850 and used since 1900 in academic circles outside the Netherlands, and by Indonesian nationalist groups. During that time the term Indo- European was already used in literature. During Dutch rule the Indos were considered Europeans possessing the Dutch nationality.

Today, the Indo Dutch are on the verge of extinction. With a couple of thousand left in Indonesia and the rest of the diaspora community scattered all over the world, they have often intermarried with other cultures in mostly the Netherlands, USA, Canada and Australia. This makes it more challenging to retain that distinct cultural identity.

Indo Dutch Cultural Traits

The acquired Indo Dutch behaviors and perceptions are a part of the blended European-Asian culture, which originated in the colonial community and was taken elsewhere and passed along through migration. For many, *being Indo Dutch* exists merely in their heart as an emotion, in their minds as memories and/or their comings and goings. When people talk about the Indo Dutch subculture, they are referring to the shared identity, which encompasses such things as traditional food, language, music, customs and beliefs, which differentiates this group from others. There is a long list of traits and customs that Indo people will immediately relate to or recognize as being typical behaviors belonging to their community.

Among the older generations (first and second generation) we see more of the typical borrowed cultural traditions (*adat*) brought from the Dutch East Indies. The main external influences on Indonesian culture have been from India and from the Middle East. The language contains many fully indigenized loanwords from Arabic and Sanskrit. Islam and Indonesian cultural traditions coexist as powerful influences in contemporary life. Both are deeply concerned with promoting correct behavior in all facets of life, with the result that moral and ethical themes are more prominent in Indonesian discourse than in contemporary Western societies. Among the more important Indonesian cultural ideas one could count: being considerate and protective of other people's feelings, showing respect and deference to parents, leaders and the elderly; the cultivation of mutual kindness and gentleness; and being well-mannered and well-spoken. We address significantly older people with oom & tante (Dutch word for uncle & aunt, even if they are not blood-related). Often we hear older people respond with "laat maar!" (Dutch for "let it be!"). This comes from *sabar* (a core virtue in traditional Indonesian culture: having the self-control to stay calm in troubling situations, letting go – having a kind of mental discipline and not acting on impulse). As my grandfather always used to say "Have inner civility" (virtues of attention, understanding, love and patience). European observers generally describe Indonesian culture as valuing refined restraint, cordiality, and sensitivity. Indonesians themselves are described as courteous, easy-going, and charming (and, less positively as fatalistic, indolent, and quick to take offense). Indos can be superstitious: for most parts of Indonesia, including Jakarta, Islam originally came from Muslim missionaries sent from India, not the Middle East. Therefore, for many Indonesians, their Islamic beliefs are mixed with mysticism and numerous superstitions. I grew up with things like: bad luck if you open an umbrella in the living room, no shoes on the coffee table (brings misery), and do not take a picture with three people (bad luck). If someone buys you perfume as a gift, you give that person a copper coin, to avoid getting into a fight. *Petjoh* is also a Dutch-based creole language that originated among the Indos. The language has influences from Dutch, Javanese and Betawi. From what I can remember it was something that was frowned upon by elders, as at home one spoke only proper Dutch. Other features include personal hygiene, like botol tjebok (use of bottled water as part of toilet etiquette and public health). Indos enjoy music, and many were raised in particular with: Krontjong, Hawaiian, Country, and Crooners, and they like jiving to Indo Rock at Indo parties. Another inherited custom is sweeping the bed with a *sapu lidih* (broom made of many wooden sticks).

One distinguishing expression of the Indo Dutch culture is making and experiencing Indo Dutch food; this is accompanied by a sociable togetherness, the generous welcoming of guests, and certain foods to eat. Indo Dutch people tend to speak about food with delight and they exhibit extensive knowledge of the products and methods of preparation. This is not so surprising when you realize that the folks who grew up in former Netherlands East Indies had constant access to food.

There was always a sweet treat to enjoy or to share, whether at home, while paying a visit to family and friends, or otherwise out in the streets, where the street vendor might pass by with satay or *kwee poetoe* (steamed coconut rice cake). There was plenty to discuss about the food from the many kitchens, which came from the various regions and islands. There was also an eager exchange of recipes and talking about food that you love so dearly, forged a bond.

Indo Dutch people are very sociable, outgoing and fond of the company of others; they are a gregarious lot. They like *gezelligheid*. This is a Dutch abstract noun (adjective form *gezellig*), which is difficult to translate in English but can best be described as an abstract sensation of individual wellbeing and joy that one typically shares with others. There is a positive and cozy atmosphere that creates this sense of belonging and togetherness that gives a feeling of warmth and contentment (*senang* is also an often used Indonesian word). Indos are generous and hospitable people, who feel no hesitation about setting an extra place at the table if an unexpected guest should happen to arrive around dinner time. Impromptu gatherings need no reason: potluck lunches, dinners and picnics often evolve from a mere suggestion. Before you know it you have a party!

"There was always a sweet treat to enjoy or to share, whether at home, or paying a visit to family and friends."

If we go farther back, the Eastern wisdom of Confucius, the social philosopher from Ancient China, is deeply rooted in the Indo Dutch philosophy. He once declared: "A person cannot be serious enough about food, as food is the force which holds society together." He put great emphasis on the art of cooking and the enjoyment of life. He demonstrated to the people how they could refine their sense of taste, and arouse their senses, to stimulate the joy of their palates. The art of cooking consists of more than just cooking in and of itself. It also includes culinary etiquette, the sociable sharing of the meal, the presentation, and the combining of various textures and flavors.

Origins of Indo Dutch Cuisine

If you are wondering what Indo Dutch food is, you are not alone. Internationally, little is known about this exotic cuisine, which is at the heart of the Indo Dutch community, and is often mistaken for Indonesian cuisine. It is not entirely wrong when you consider it originated in the same geographical area now known as Indonesia. But in my opinion this is an oversimplification. There are distinct differences between the two, even though they are intertwined on many levels. The relationship looks complicated. The same assumption is made about the Indo Dutch people who have roots in the former Dutch East Indies, and are often mistaken for Indonesian (that notion is reinforced because of the term in English: Dutch-Indonesian). Therefore, in my book, I prefer to use the term Indo Dutch (like 'Indo Belanda' as they call it in Indonesia).

Even in the Netherlands, when it comes to Indo Dutch food, terms like *Indisch, Indonesisch* and *Chinees-Indisch* are used interchangeably

(and incorrectly). There is confusion and unfortunately a lack of historical awareness. These cuisines all deserve to be recognized on their own merits, as they have evolved slightly differently. It's like the analogy: 'All apples are fruits but not all fruits are apples.' How did our cuisine evolve? Can we talk about the subject of colonialism without raising too many eyebrows? I think we can when we put the emphasis on food. Part of the reason I wrote this book is for people to understand and recognize the differences and for the Indo Dutch cooking style to receive the accolades it so richly deserves.

The identity of a cuisine is determined by elements like: history, geography, religion, ethnic diversity, culinary etiquette, predominant flavors and authentic recipes - with reference to ingredients, cooking techniques and presentation.

When we look at Indonesia for instance, we usually don't talk about just Indonesian cuisine, we refer to the regions and ethnic groups that have their own cooking style, like Sumatra, Bali, Java (East, West, Betawi, Djokja), Manado, Madura and Chinese Indonesian etc.

Indo Dutch is one of the oldest Eurasian fusion cuisines. It is an ethnic cuisine, belonging to the culinary heritage of the Indo Dutch diaspora, a hybrid community that emerged in the former Dutch East Indies (modern Indonesia). The Indo Dutch cooking style encompasses a wide variety of typical regional and traditional dishes native to Indonesia, the Netherlands and a fusion of both, represented in a diverse culinary repertoire that evolved over a period of more than 350 years. This overlap with reference to Indo Dutch and Indonesian cuisine (also attributing to confusion) is caused by adoption of Indo Dutch dishes into Indonesian cuisine and vice versa. For instance the *rijsttafel* is served there as "typical" Indonesian.

It is an amalgamation of the best things from each of the two cultures. Hundreds of years ago, Dutch colonialists in remote locations had to substitute ingredients in order to replicate the taste of home as closely as possible. Thus, European recipes were transformed or improved with local spices, and European methods of preparation were adapted and applied to local ingredients. Indigenous dishes, for their part, were influenced by a variety of cultures: China, India, the Arab world, and enriched by European elements of countries such as Portugal, England, France and The Netherlands. New products were already being brought over by the Spanish and Portuguese traders and explorers, prior to the Dutch merchants colonizing the entire archipelago. The Spanish carried over the red peppers and potatoes from South America, and introduced those to Europe in the second half of the 16th century. European traders transported these new ingredients to areas and ports around the world. Peanuts from South America were used for peanut sauce for gado-gado and satay. Cassava from the Caribbean gave Maluku and Irian Jaya their main product. The Dutch imported cabbage, cauliflower, carrots, long beans, potatoes and corn.

The Indo Dutch cooking style demonstrates resourcefulness and is known for the lavish use of spices and ingredients of both worlds, which renders them Indo Dutch to the palate. The wide variation of dishes with an abundance of flavors sets each dish apart, no matter how simple. For example: rijsttafel (an elaborate meal of Indonesian and Indo Dutch dishes), Indische macaroni schotel (baked mac 'n cheese Indo style), Indische huzarensalade (Russian salad Indies style), spekkoek (spice layer cake), klappertaart (coconut tart), ajam smoor (braised chicken with spices), Indische pastei toetoep (Indies shepherds pie), ajam kodok (stuffed chicken), split pea soup with rice, perkedel (meat balls or meatloaf Indo style), just to name a few. Many of these dishes and food customs can be found in both Indonesia and the Netherlands, mostly within family circles, traditional recipes passed down for generations. The Indo Dutch cuisine further evolved in the respective countries, with local ingredients and cooking styles, while staying true to authentic tastes.

When people hear *fusion* they often think hip, fun and fresh. For the Indo Dutch people it is their cooking style, the result of hundreds of years of layering different cultures, and new fused with the old. Other examples of fusion cuisines are Anglo-Indian, Peranakan or Nonya cuisine (blend of Chinese and Malay cooking), Vietnamese-French, Cristang Cuisine, (Malacca Portuguese, Dutch, Indonesian), Eurasian (Malaysia,Singapore), Yoshuko (Japanese- Western), Macanese Cuisine (Chinese-Portuguese).

"Though the name of the cuisine refers to a different period and a country that no longer exists, the people and their food culture that came from there still do."

When we talk about Indo Dutch food we not only visit another world, we also visit another time, just like Constantinople instead of Istanbul, Bombay instead of Mumbay, Indochina instead of Vietnam. Though the name of the cuisine refers to a different period and a country that no longer exists, the people and their food culture that came from there still do. It is a legacy that is cherished, that has evolved, and is shared with both Indonesia and Holland and is passed on by the Indo Dutch community.

Dutch Eating Habits in the Tropics

In the beginning, during the colonial time, Dutch eating habits were different from the traditional Indo Dutch eating habits. For the average Dutch person, the purpose of food was primarily to nourish the body and soul. Three meals a day were consumed at regular times of the day. Families would gather together at these times. However, for the inhabitants of former Dutch East Indies, togetherness and sociability also played an important role. Whenever you were hungry was when you would eat. Many dishes were prepared in such a way that they would keep for long periods of time. Food was left out on the table and eaten at room temperature.

In due time, these practices were quickly adopted by the Dutch people who lived there. The Dutch structure of the meal had to be left behind. Raised on bread, potatoes, meat, fish and vegetables, they discovered alternative substitutes and exotic ingredients. The European recipes were improved with local seasonings. Additionally, there were several dishes per category, such as meat, vegetables and side dishes. In this way, European dishes with an Asian core were created.

Another adopted custom is the selamatan, a communal feast from Java, symbolizing the social unity of those participating in it. The feast is common among the closely related Javanese, Sundanese and Madurese people. A selamatan can be given to celebrate almost any event, including birth, marriage, death, moving to a new house etc. The ceremony takes its name from the Javanese word slamet, from

Arabic: salam, which refers to a peaceful state of equanimity, in which nothing will happen. This is what the host intends for both himself and his guests, by experiencing the egalitarian structure of the selametan and the petitions of supernatural protection from spirits.

The Indo Dutch cuisine is actually a wonderful culinary translation of *Unity in Diversity* (Bhinneka Tunggal Ika) a sacred phrase by Mpu Tantular, a 14th century poet sage of the Majapahit Empire; a reflection of the community, multifaceted heritage and cultures, lifestyle and food customs of those who came to this large archipelago and settled there, strongly influenced by indigenous and European infused elements. Whereas Bhinneka Tunggal Ika originated from the principle tenet of *gotong royong* (working together towards a common goal; cooperation), Indonesian and Indo Dutch culinary customs stem from the tradition of communal eating; one dish for all. In due course, the Dutch discovered this principle and created the *rijsttafel* tradition.

A typical colonial meal in the tropics during the 19th century: For breakfast: nasi goreng (fried rice). For lunch - the principal meal of the day: *rijsttafel* served at room temperature, followed by steak & potatoes. Teatime - around 4pm: savory pastries & little sweet snacks. Supper or a light meal late in the evening – leftovers from lunch. Throughout the day food hawkers would come by the house and sell anything from ingredients to complete meals. After more Dutch women arrived in the Indies, a greater variety of Dutch/European food appeared on the menu.

Rijsttafel

If you had asked me as a child who had invented *rijsttafel* (literally means rice table), I would have answered full of confidence, "My Oma!" And nobody would have been able to convince me otherwise, if you were speaking about the *rijsttafel,* which was served in our restaurant.

In the course of time, I have had to modify my story somewhat, when, out of curiosity, I stumbled upon other facts surrounding this traditional meal. The way I heard it from my grandparents was that in the former Dutch East Indies, where they grew up, the mid-day meal was a hot lunch. This was often a simple meal, with rice at its focal point, and some side dishes. For special occasions, this was enhanced and alternated with dozens of side dishes. This *rijsttafel* was served by experienced and beloved *kokkies* (as these cooks in home service were called).

As was typical amongst European royalty, people employed legions of servants, and abundant banquets were thrown to flaunt their wealth and power. In the Dutch East Indies, at the homes of the affluent white Europeans, merchants and plantation owners, abundant dinners were hosted, where they served up impressive *rijsttafels* with as many fragrant and beautiful dishes as possible. This increased the social status of the host. The *rijsttafel* gained popularity amongst the European elite, particularly during the second half of the nineteenth century. Out in the countryside, this was entrusted to the women who were in service in the kitchen. They were familiar with the local traditions (such as *selamatans*), and the daily menu would often contain mostly rice with side dishes. Wherever the master of the house would move or travel to, he would bring his kokkie, and she expanded her culinary repertoire with the regional ethnic recipes she picked up from her peers.

As the story goes, the name *rijsttafel* was given by a Dutch chef working for a well known Indo European Hotel *Des Indes*, in the former Dutch East Indies in the 19th century. The name could be derived from the Dutch equivalent banquet *Brabantse koffietafel* (literally means coffee table Brabant style); an elaborate buffet consisting of all kinds of breads, cold cuts, cheeses, bread spreads and served with coffee and tea. During its centuries of popularity in Dutch East Indies, lines of servants or sarong-clad waitresses ceremoniously served the marathon meal on platters laden with steaming bowls of fragrant foods. The first item to be served was a cone-shaped pile of rice on a large platter, which the server placed in the center of the table. The servers then surrounded the rice platter with as many as 40 small bowls holding meat and vegetable dishes as well as condiments.

When you read about the *Indische** rijsttafel, you will find a divergence of definitions: from *rijsttafel-ing* as an art, a reflection of a refined and discerning food culture, to an overabundant interpretation of an Indo Dutch meal. It is a little too black-and-white to suggest that it was only the Indo Dutch elite (amongst whom the plantation owners and merchants) who stood at the cradle of this festive meal. The origin of the *rijsttafel* is much more colorful and was exposed to many different influences.

According to famous Indo intellectual and writer Jan Boon aka Tjalie Robinson, the development of the *rijsttafel* began in the time of the Portuguese, a century before the Dutch arrived in Indonesia. The Portuguese lived all over Southeast Asia. When they were reassigned elsewhere, they brought along their favorite dishes, often because their favorite kitchen maid (or *baboe*) traveled with them. As is well-known among the *Indo Dutchmen*, the loyal *kokkie* picked up cooking tips all over: recipes from the local ethnic delicatessen, and also from colleagues. Whoever had a beloved *kokkie*, with years of loyal service, had a real living cookbook at their fingertips. Thanks to intercultural marriages and through cultural exchanges, people ate "anything and everything." More and more, the *rijsttafel* began to take shape.

These beloved *kokkies* understood the art of cooking and should rightly be regarded as vanguards. They had the knowledge of the exotic products, herbs and preservatives. As a result of the development of improved heat sources and stoves, the contribution of new cooking techniques and cookbooks, the availability of new ingredients, and the creativity of the *kokkie*, the *rijsttafel* was refined even further. The composition of the various dishes was partly determined by the variation among the population from the many regions of the archipelago. At that time, there was already a notion of "food culture". There was extensive trade in prepared foods. You could eat anywhere, until late into the night. Street vendors would come by your house with small portable kitchens, and you would see them all over the towns with items from simple snacks to complete meals. Long-distance business travelers became familiar with the *waroengs* (soup kitchens), where ready-made meals were available: rice with side dishes, conveniently wrapped in a banana leaf. Many communities and cultures have had influence on the origin of the *rijsttafel* as we know it now. "Indonesianized" Chinese ingredients such as *mie* (noodles), pork and soy sauce enriched the *rijsttafel*. In addition, the Dutch (who could not get used to the dietary laws of Islam), Arabs, Indians (from India), Spanish, British, and not least the native Indonesians themselves, all contributed in their own manner to the tradition of the *rijsttafel*. The *rijsttafel* is now also known as a national Dutch dish as well as an Indonesian one. After the *rijsttafel* began gaining acclaim, thanks in part to tourism, it became apparent that international honor could be achieved. Therefore the title Dutch was better than the word *Indische** which could be confused with "Indian", for example. Ultimately, it deserves the title "Indonesian", since this feast was conceived in Indonesia, and could simply not be perfected without the Indonesian raw materials and cooking expertise. I agree with Tjalie Robinson that the *rijsttafel* ought to be called Indo Dutch *rijsttafel*. And to be historically and ethnically correct, *rijsttafel* is the cultural treasure of the Indo-community, a delicious asset of a blended culture and one of the finest triumphs of *former colonial Indonesia*.

Naturally, many combinations are possible, and it can be made as extensive as you wish. Regular customers gladly left the selection to the host or hostess. Depending on the time available, a rijsttafel can be simple or very elaborate. Most side dishes, especially the meats and sauces, can be assembled the day before. This has the added advantage of the seasoning deepening over time, and the dish being even tastier. On the day itself, all you have to do is prepare the vegetables and boil the rice. The prepared dish can be warmed up in a heatproof container in the oven or microwave, just prior to serving.

A *rijsttafel for one*, served on one plate, is called *nasi rames*. Rice in the middle surrounded by various dishes; sambal goreng dishes (dry-cooked spicy meat and/or vegetables), some serundeng, atjar and krupuk, and completed with satay ajam or babi and a small bowl of sajur lodeh. Since this is plated in the kitchen all at once, there is no personal choice of side dishes, and the meal can be consumed more quickly.

There was a Netherlands Indies Restaurant in San Francisco in 1939. Could this be the first time the west coast was introduced to East Indies Cuisine? The Isle of Bali restaurant participated in the 1939 Golden Gate International Exposition held in San Francisco, California. At the time, the Isle of Bali was billed as a Netherlands Indies Restaurant, but today the Netherlands Indies is known as Indonesia. The Isle of Bali served Javanese cuisine with locations in San Francisco, Paris, Brussels and The Hague (Den Haag). On the menu: special *curry* dishes – referring to the *boemboe or spice mix base* for dishes such as nasi goreng – fried rice with a curry base. Then a selection of RIJSTTAFELS – from 9 to 14 and more dishes served with rice. There was an assortment of A LA CARTE dishes such as sajoers or soups served with the main course, pork, beef, and sambalans - spicy relish base with added ingredients. Then there were the chicken dishes and various dishes, like: steamed rice, gado-gado, kroepoek, fried egg etc. And last but not least desserts: fried bananas, Javanese rice porridge, coconut with Javanese sugar and special ice cream.

Indisch(e)—is a Dutch adjective for 'Indies' or' Indo Dutch', pertaining to the colonial mixed culture of the former Dutch East Indies.

First Indo Dutch Cookbooks

Legislation initially prohibited Dutch men from bringing European women to the Indies. Around mid 19th century more European women started to come to the Dutch Indies. Different climate and new way of life required knowledge and appropriate adjustments, especially related to household affairs. In many affluent Indo Dutch homes, the lady of the house very seldom troubled herself with domestic chores, preferring to delegate them to her servant. The *kokkie* (the female cook) received instructions from the lady of the house about what was for dinner. During those times scores of recipe books were written and published, along with detailed instructions on how to circumvent many pitfalls that could confront a kokkie. Most cookbooks came from colonial women with time on their hands. One of the first Indies cookbooks is titled *Kokkie Bitja* or *Kitab Masak Masakan India*, published in Batavia in 1856. It is a collection of short Indonesian, Chinese and even Dutch recipes, written in hybrid Malay mixed with Dutch words – as can be seen from recipe names like *kwe tulband*, *pastij oedang*, or *stoof ayam*. The title Kokkie Bitja, *Beloved Cook*, refers to the author, a certain *Nonna* (Miss) Cornelia, living at the *Tiada- Katahoewan* estate. We know very little about her, only that she suddenly passed away in 1856 only days before publication of the reprint, after a nervous fit in the kitchen while failing her *kwee broeder* cake, as the publishers tell us. Another popular book is that of Mrs Catenius van der Meijden, a writer and collector of indigenous recipes. She was instrumental in providing knowledge to European women who migrated to the Indies. During her stay in Java Mrs. Van der Meijden had successfully collected thousands of rijsttafel and European recipes, used as a kind of manual for European women in the Indies. (see pictures)

Indo Dutch Cooking Abroad

After the Second World War, and once Indonesian independence was a done deal, Indo Dutch people were forced to migrate to The Netherlands. They brought with them the Indo Dutch cuisine, their tastes and eating habits. The special meals being prepared and eaten were a practical manner of embodying a personal culture and a strong longing for the flavors and fragrances of the former Dutch East-Indies. Cooking for fellow Indo Dutch acquaintances, sharing their misfortune, was done with pleasure, and people found solace by coming together in companionship and sharing a meal.

Indo Dutch women were renowned for their resourcefulness and creativity in the kitchen. Despite a lack of fresh Asian ingredients, they found substitutes, and thus a new fusion was created, Indo Dutch dishes with a Western core: Indo Dutch cuisine evolved once again. At that time, The Netherlands was not a country with an extensive culinary, gastronomical tradition. The Dutch kitchen was more of a country kitchen. The Dutch were not very adventurous when it came to food. Simple, available and nutritious were the words associated with the "average" Dutchman. Going out to eat was also not commonly done, because of the cost: The Netherlands was in a period of reconstruction. This changed during the 1960s when the economy had recovered, personal wealth increased, and tourism grew. Because of this, the traveling Dutchman now became acquainted with other European food cultures, and developed an interest for tasty foreign food such as Italian, French and Spanish, as well as for the exotic cuisine from South East Asia.

One of Oma's proudest achievements is that she once prepared a meal for the Sultan of Pontianak, who was staying at the Hotel Des Indes. As Oma tells it: "The Sultan of Pontianak was staying at the Hotel Des Indes, and it was said they served very good Indo Dutch food there too. All those djongossen (servers) came along with platters of food, one after the other, to serve the rijsttafel. Then at a certain time, his car was at our door. And they asked me if I could provide food. I made the food at home, and it was picked up."

During the 1960s and 1970s there were a number of Indo Dutch family restaurants, mostly to cater to their own community, in California. My dad's sister Tante Adje and her husband Oom Ton Verkouteren opened Sarina's Inn on Foothill Boulevard in La Crescenta. Their three kids, Gerry, Elly and Michael helped out. Cooking Indonesian food was not always easy, because specific ingredients were hard to find. There was an Asian grocery store in Chinatown in Los Angeles, where most of the community met on the weekends and of course one had to be resourceful and use substitutes. Some were so fortunate to have family or friends from Holland bring an extra suitcase full of spices.

The Indo Dutch people celebrate all the feasts in the Christian calendar, and bring in the New Year western style. From an Indo Dutch point of view, the more the merrier!

Similar Cuisines in Holland

In The Netherlands, we still see the terms *Indonesisch, Indisch and Chinees-Indisch* (Indonesian, Indies and Chinese-Indies) mixed up and bandied about, which causes much confusion. Although these cuisines appear similar, they each underwent different evolutions, and as such, deserve their separate places in the culinary history of The Netherlands.

CHINESE INDIES CUISINE

The number of Indies grocery stores (tokos) and restaurants grew principally in The Hague. However, it was Oma who popularized authentic Indo Dutch cuisine in the capital city of Amsterdam. At first, the better parts of her customers were students and people who enjoyed Indo Dutch food out of a sense of nostalgia. In due course, more and more Dutch people became interested in the tastes of ethnic cuisine, and gave the strong- flavored dishes a try. However, for many Dutch people, the Indo Dutch food was too spicy. Oma always said, *"We won't make concessions!"* She didn't feel it was necessary to pander to Dutch taste buds.

This gave the already-established Chinese restaurateurs the lucrative chance to respond to the evolving Dutch eating habits and the increased demand for Indo Dutch (Indies) food. Indo Dutch-inspired dishes began appearing on the menus of Chinese restaurants. To make the transition easier, they did acquiesce to the plea of the Dutch: less strongly flavored and spicy food, and larger portions. Granted, the dishes were mostly prepared with Chinese cooking methods using less labor-intensive stir-fried dishes. Indo Dutch dishes were given a Chinese twist; they were in fact somewhat bastardized: more oil, fewer seasonings, and the dishes were cooked fast and short, and adjusted for Dutch palates. As an example, satay was deep-fried instead of grilled. Things even went so far that it was commonly thought that *nasi goreng* with ham and a fried egg was an authentic Chinese dish. Many Chinese take-out restaurants added "-Indisch" after the word "Chinees". And this is the origin of a new Asian fusion cuisine in The Netherlands.

Oma again: *"Indo Dutch food, there are so many differences. We have the true Indo Dutch cuisine. Ours differs from Chinese-Indies, where it's common to season like the Dutch, and a lot of oil is used. We buy our spices here, imported, preferably fresh, like laos, jahe and all those other things we need, fresh and pricey from Suriname. A Chinese-Indies restaurant is the same as a Bulgarian-Icelandic restaurant: that really can't exist. Unless it's a Chinese- Indo Dutch person, born in Indonesia. And only if he cooks as it was done back there."*

INDONESIAN CUISINE

This cuisine underwent a different evolution. The country is made up of thousands of islands and regions, each with its own cooking style, based upon their own ethnic culture and religion. However, Indonesian cuisine is also influenced by other countries, not only the ingredients, but also cooking techniques. Strictly speaking, one can only refer to Indonesian cuisine when in the country itself, with access to its genuine, fresh ingredients. When canned or dried goods are used, it already tastes different. But now, in The Netherlands for instance, many ingredients from the authentic Indonesian kitchen are available both fresh and frozen. Over the course of time, Indo Dutch restaurant owners turned more and more towards authentic Indonesian cuisine. This was how they strove to distinguish themselves from Chinees-Indisch restaurants, and prove that they would not make concessions to the authentic flavors, which the people in Indonesia were accustomed to. The popularity of Indonesian cuisine outside the country's borders can also be traced back to the forced emigration of the Indo Dutch population, as well as an increase in Indonesian restaurants owned by Indonesian immigrants.

The best Indonesian restaurants can be found in The Netherlands, aside from those in Indonesia itself. For its part, the Indonesian kitchen has also influenced cuisines in other countries. One popular dish, for example, is satay. This delicacy has found its way to the peninsula of Malaysia, and spread farther north to become one of Thailand's favorite dishes. One also doesn't come across many other Asian menus without *rendang* or sambal. Traditionally, appetizers were not generally known; instead, all dishes were served as one course. Even the *soto* (soup) was to be enjoyed alongside the main course. The fundamental herbs and spices of the dishes are the same as those in Indo Dutch cuisine, but they are fresh, local versions. Strangely enough, we find that seasonings such as nutmeg, cloves and mace -- the foundation of centuries of spice trade -- are seldom used in traditional Indonesian cuisine. However, we do discover them in Indo Dutch cuisine. Worldwide Indonesia does not yet enjoy as much fame as Thai cuisine for instance. Since 2012 the Indonesian Tourism and Creative Economy Ministry has set 30 iconic dishes as part of a culinary diplomacy initiative that should represent their rich culinary heritage.

JAVA

Java is influenced by colonial history as well as by the Arab World, India, China and European countries such as Portugal, England and The Netherlands. The Javanese were accustomed to sautéed and stir-fried dishes prepared in the wok, a Chinese practice. The Dutch wanted beef stew, and that was enhanced with spices, creating braised dishes (*smoor*). From the Portuguese came the custom of marinating meat and baking it in the oven. The Javanese do not generally eat much meat, and as such, we can find many vegetarian dishes prepared with soy -- tofu and tempeh -- besides a variety of dishes made with chicken.

The West-Javanese (Sundanese) kitchen is sharply seasoned, but not as spicy as on Sumatra, Pandang cuisine. Many fresh and raw ingredients are used, such as *lalab* with sambal and *karedok* (raw vegetable salad). Other typical dishes are: sajur asam, lotek, sambal terasi, tumis taotjo, empal gepuk, gulai kambing, es duren and es cendol.

Betawi cuisine -- originating from the era when Jakarta was still known as Batavia: nasi uduk, ketoprak, gado-gado betawi and kerak telor. East-Javanese cuisine includes more meat in its repertoire, and the dishes are somewhat sweeter due to the well-known Javanese palm sugar: *gula jawa*. In addition, fish-based products are used more often in cooking, such as *terasi* and *petis*. This cuisine has been strongly influenced by the island of Madura: soto and ajam madura.

On Central Java, dishes are even sweeter. Djokja is famous for its gudek with jackfruit, ajam goreng, and klepon. Dishes that can also be found on Central Java are items such as bakso, lumpia semarang, serabi and wingko babat. In addition, other well-known dishes are petjil, lotek, gudek, ajam opor, sajur lodeh, rawon, bebotok and tumpeng.

SULAWESI

The Minahasan and Manadoan cuisines from North-Sulawesi (formerly known as North Celebes) are notable for its use of meat and fish. This cuisine is influenced by the Dutch; for example, the dish known as *brenebon* ("bruine boon" or brown bean): a pork casserole seasoned with nutmeg and cloves. There is also *sup brenebon* (brown bean soup). Other more exotic dishes contain dog meat, rat or bat.

SUMATRA

West Sumatra is known for its Padang (Minangkabau) cuisine, which is relatively spicy. The liberal use of peppers is tempered with a generous addition of coconut milk. Here you will find fewer vegetables, and more beef dishes on the menu. At the popular restaurants of West Sumatra, fare from the kitchen of Minangkabau is served. The table is covered in little plates and bowls with dishes served at room temperature. You only pay for what you have eaten.

Northern Sumatra: cuisine from the Atjeh region was influenced by merchants from India, Arabia and Persia. Popular dishes are rendang and kalio (similar to rendang, but more diluted and lighter in color). This cuisine is also notable for curry dishes such as kare or guleh. Dishes such as dendeng, babi panggang, karo and toba can also frequently be found on the menu. Southern Sumatra is responsible for Palembang cuisine: Pindang is the cooking style used here.

BALI

Balinese cuisine is famous for babi guling (spit-roast suckling pig) and bebek betutu (duck meat steamed in banana leaves, then grilled).

INDO DUTCH INFLUENCE IN HOLLAND'S NATIONAL CUISINE

The craving for Indo Dutch food has influenced traditional Dutch cooking. Many Indo Dutch elements have since been adopted and assimilated into everyday Dutch cuisine such as bami goreng and nasi goreng. Nasi goreng (fried rice) is originally a dish in which leftovers (rice and meat) were stir-fried in a wok, and served for breakfast. In The Netherlands, we usually treat it as a main dinner dish. Every self-respecting snackbar has the *nasibal* and *bamischijf* on their menu. Naturally, the peanut sauce for the fries is essential

as well. Many dishes are enhanced with herbs, spices and sambal. Spicy food is eaten often, just as people were used to doing in the former colony, the Dutch East Indies. Indo Dutch *rijstttafel* has been established as belonging to the unique culinary Dutch repertoire. Dutch people proudly serve this festive meal to their foreign visitors. As such, the Dutch can be named the rightful ambassadors of Indo Dutch and Indonesian cuisine. Since January of 2016, the rijsttafel has officially become part of Dutch intangible cultural heritage.

Indo Dutch cuisine was also influenced and enriched by other countries.

ENGLISH: shepherd's pie—*pastei tutup*, pasteitje – Cornish pasty-*small sealed pastries*, stuffed chicken—*ajam kodok*

PORTUGUESE: dried fish—*bacalhou* (cod) – risolles

SPANISH: empanadas—*panada* - small sealed pastries

ARABIC: *martabak – kebab*

INDIAN: curries

CHINESE: *babi panggang—fu yung hai—pangsit/wonton—chop suey*—many stir-fried and rice dishes

DUTCH: potato-based dishes & ground beef *frikadel, smoor* (braised dishes) soups like *split pea soup with rice* and *brown bean soup,* many pastries and sweets, like *spekkoek, klappertaart* etc.

INDO DUTCH ETIQUETTE

Eating Indo Dutch food is something you have to learn to do. You could call it Indo Dutch food with instructions. In the early years of the restaurant, some uninformed patrons would mix together everything that was on their plate and pour over the peanut sauce, as though it were a trusty stew with gravy. It may have been a comforting Dutch habit, but disastrous to the Indo Dutch meal, and a grave dishonor to do it. I'm sure it was also deeply dismaying to the chef, who had prepared her uniquely flavored dishes with great care. Besides not talking with your mouth full and not "mixing cement," as my auntie used to say (drinking in between bites), a few other table manners were ingrained in me. How should it be done? Let's examine proper Indo Dutch table manners.

WHAT TIME DO WE EAT?

It was customary in Western countries to gather as a family at three particular times of the day to eat together. What the Indo Dutch adopted from the indigenous people was the habit of eating at any time of day. In Western and Central Indonesia, the cooking was traditionally done in the latter part of the morning, and then set out around noon. Many families do not have a predetermined lunchtime. Consequently, most dishes are suitable for eating throughout the day, even if they have been on the table for several hours. These same dishes will then be reheated for the evening meal. A variety of condiments are provided to accompany almost every dish. Naturally, there is always something to nibble on, a sweet or savory tidbit to satisfy the appetite for a snack.

SERVING

Rice is served in a large open tureen, placed in the center of the table; *sajurs* (the wet-vegetable dishes) and soups in a bowl, and the meat, chicken and/or fish items on a platter. Other items on the table will be *sambal*, *atjar* (pickled vegetables) in a bottle or jar, a bottle of *ketjap manis* (sweet soy sauce) and *krupuk* (deep fried crackers).

HANDS OR SILVERWARE?

At our house, and in many Indo Dutch restaurants, the table is set with a deep (soup) dish, and a spoon and fork are used for eating. A spoon is useful, as "wet" dishes such as *sajurs*, braised dishes and soup are served. Hold the spoon in the right hand, and the fork in the left. Rice is eaten with a spoon, so you taste more of the sauce. A knife can be used as well, to cut the larger pieces of vegetables and meat. Sometimes just a spoon is sufficient, when seated on the sofa, plate in the left hand and spoon in the right.

To eat with your hands, make a small ball of rice using four fingers, and dip this in a little sauce, then pop it in your mouth using your thumb as a lever. An important rule of dining etiquette is to use only the right hand, as the left is used for personal hygiene after using the restroom. Do not put your hand into a dish that is being shared communally; instead, use the serving spoon with your left hand. Wash your hands well, before and after eating. It is customary to provide a finger bowl with water and lemon at each place setting to rinse off your hands.

WHERE DO WE BEGIN?

If white rice is being served, it is customary to begin with that. Place a mound of rice in the center of a deep plate. Arrange several warm and cold side dishes around the rice like a wreath. The sauce from the wet dishes can be poured over the rice. Each individual dish can be eaten with some rice. Begin with the mildest dish and end with

the spiciest. Place a spoonful of the homemade sambal, often served alongside, at the edge of your plate (sambal badjak, taotjo orterasi).

Main dishes are often served lukewarm, whereby the seasonings and ingredients can better come into their own. Only the rice is served steaming hot. However, in The Netherlands it is more common to eat all the dishes warm. If necessary, keep the dishes warm using a hot plate. For larger groups, it is easiest to serve everything buffet-style, so that people can either eat at the table, place the plate on their laps, or hold them in their hands.

MOUTH ON FIRE?

At our restaurant, we always had two very spicy dishes: *bebotok* and *obloh-obloh*. If everything is mixed together, then not only is the unique flavor of the individual dishes lost, but everything will become equally spicy.

When eating *pedis* (spicy or hot) food, do not drink water, beer or wine to put out the fire! This will only aggravate the burning sensation. Try taking a bite of rice, krupuk, cucumber, milk or yogurt, or suck on a sugar cube.

"Indo Dutch food has become a local Dutch custom, because everyone eats it now. Even people who have never been to Indonesia sometimes like it spicier than I do! You wouldn't believe it… I always say: 'Ladies and gentlemen, please remember not to mix and mash your food, because if it's too hot, you'll hit the roof! I would get a lovely chandelier though…' But I do always warn them beforehand, otherwise they'd grumble, wouldn't they? And then they would say, 'I'm not paying for this, I didn't ask for it to be so spicy.' While they had indeed asked for that! But they do have to pay after all, I'm very strict with them. 'You must pay, because there's only a little bit left on your plate, so where did the rest of it go, then?'"

—*Oma*

TOOLS & TECHNIQUES

TOOLS & TECHNIQUES

Cooking Tools

Below you will find a short description of cooking materials and methods traditionally used in Indo Dutch cuisine. Having these available will make the preparation of the dishes easier.

COBEK AND ULEKAN (MORTAR AND PESTLE)

These are used for *ulek-ing* (crushing, grinding, pulverizing) herbs, or making *bumbu* (a mixture of herbs or chili paste) in a *cobek* (shallow, stone mortar about eight inches in diameter).

Tip: Soak a new mortar in water mixed with two tablespoons of salt for seven days to remove any loose grit. Rub the stone mortar all over with fresh coconut *(or coconut oil)* and leave for thirty minutes. The coconut oil will be absorbed and form a proper protective layer. Rinse the mortar with plain warm water; avoid using dish soap, as this will be absorbed by the stone. The use of a mortar and pestle is suitable for a small amount of ingredients.

FOOD PROCESSOR

A food processor is practical and helps you save time. It is used for grinding herbs and spices, which can then be used for making bumbus. A food processor will chop and slice them into a microscopic mince, while a mortar and pestle will crush and smear the ingredients into a paste. Besides the textural difference produced by the two methods, a partial emulsification of the water-based constituents into the oil occurs with the food processor.

PROCEDURE FOR MAKING *BUMBUS* USING A *MORTAR AND PESTLE*

These herb or chili paste mixtures are the foundation of most Indo Dutch dishes. Onions, garlic and *sambal* are crushed together in a mortar. The herb mixture can then be sautéed in oil, together with the main components of fish, meat, poultry, and/or vegetables, then simmered with a small amount of liquid such as *santan* (coconut milk).

Peel the ingredients, where necessary, and chop them finely before using the *tjobek/chobek* and *ulekan*, so it is easier to pulverize them. The pestle is used by moving the wrist with short back-and-forth motions onto the mortar. This allows the aromatic essential oils to be released. The ingredients are mashed together to form a smooth paste.

CHINESE CLEAVER

This versatile tool looks like a butcher's knife, but is much lighter. This multi- purpose all-in-one-knife can be used to peel ginger or bone out a chicken. The flat blade can smash garlic and the spine can pound meat. It can also be used to create paper thin slices of carrot and remove skin from a fish. A great alternative to the good old 8-inch chef's knife.

WOK OR *WAJAN*

A wok or *wajan* is a round-bottomed pan, similar to a half ball. The wok stems from Chinese cuisine and has one long, wooden handle. A wajan is used in Indonesian and Indo Dutch cuisine and is distinctive for its two handles, also known as ears. The wajan derives its name from the Indonesian word *waja*, meaning steel. They are also available in other materials such as cast iron, enamel, carbon steel and stainless steel, as well as electric and non-stick varieties. A wok is suitable for stir- frying, braising, stewing, steaming or frying (it uses less oil than a regular frying pan). It is designed in such a way that it warms up and maintains its heat evenly. Because of the sloping sides, it is easy to toss food during stir-frying, as the food will always fall back towards the center of the pan, the hottest part. Moreover, the pan is convenient for making braised or stewed dishes, which have a lot of moisture at the start of the cooking process, and are left with a thick sauce.

A lightweight cast iron or enamel wajan with a diameter of approximately twelve to fourteen inches is recommended. An electric wok or a wok with non-stick coating cannot always reach the high temperatures needed for searing meat quickly and keeping vegetables crisp. These types of pans are more useful for stews.

A FLAT OR ROUND BOTTOM?

Do you use a gas stove? Then you can use the traditional wok with a round bottom. Place a wok ring around the burner for stability. If you have an electric or ceramic cooktop, you may choose to use the flat-bottom wok or a sauté pan. The disadvantage of these types of pans is that it is difficult to make natural, smooth stir- frying motions, and that they require more oil. An alternative solution is to use a separate gas stove just for the wok. Keep the wok in a convenient place and in plain sight so you will use it more often.

SUTIL, SODET, SPIDER

When cooking in a wajan, use a *sutil*, a long-handled spatula with a flat metal scoop, which can be found in a variety of types and sizes. You could also use a wooden spatula with a slightly angled edge. These are useful for cooking and frying in a wajan, but you could of course use any other similar utensil as well. A *sodet* is a flat wooden spoon for scooping rice. Another essential utensil is a wire mesh skimmer, also called a spider. This is used to remove and drain food from a pan after frying or blanching.

KITCHEN TONGS

When cooking I use this utensil to grip, lift and rotate food with delicate precision.

STEAMERS

Who can live without an electric rice steamer these days? An electric rice cooker is very practical for larger amounts, in addition to keeping the rice warm. Steamers for gas or electric stovetops are also available.

Kukusan: A cone-shaped basket inside a copper or aluminum pan with a lid, for steaming rice.

Bamboo steaming basket with lid: this type of steamer is placed inside the wajan over boiling water. Bamboo steamers are preferable over metal ones, as they absorb moisture rather than dripping the moisture back into the food.

ALUMINUM

Many Indo Dutch dishes contain acidic ingredients such as lemon or tamarind juice and coconut milk. Aluminum pots and pans could cause a chemical reaction or discoloration. It is also not recommended to use aluminum foil for covering food on metal hot plates. The chemical reaction that can be triggered could make the food taste bitter.

Cooking Methods

Indo Dutch cooking methods are similar to Asian and Western cuisine, in particular when it comes to basic techniques such as stir-frying, searing, blanching, deep frying, braising, stewing, simmering and steaming. The following is a description of some commonly used methods.

STIR-FRYING

When stir-frying, the ingredients are continually tossed and turned in the pan as the lowest part of the wajan is the hottest. Scoop everything from the center outwards. Stir-frying should be done quickly to prevent the food from becoming limp or sticking to the sides of the pan. To begin, heat the dry wajan until it is quite hot. To test whether the pan is at the right temperature, sprinkle a few drops of water onto it; if it is hot enough, the water droplets will bounce around *(and evaporate)*. Only then, add a small amount of oil *(and swirl it around)*. When the oil begins to smoke very slightly, it is hot enough. Make sure that the oil reaches up the sides of the pan. When stir-frying aromatics such as garlic, onion, red pepper or ginger, the pan should not be too hot *(otherwise they will become bitter)*. For meat and vegetables, the pan should be quite hot, however, as this will create that nice crisp outer crust. A few other well-known cooking methods and terms you will encounter in Indo Dutch cuisine are searing, deep frying, grilling, simmering, braising, stewing, steaming (*kukus*), blanching, au bain marie, binding, softening, garnishing or dressing, marinating, breading, roasting, puréeing, and so on.

WRAPPING

Some dishes are wrapped in spring roll or wonton wrappers, or in filo dough. There are also dishes which can be wrapped in aluminum foil or plastic wrap (for example, *lemper*), as well as banana leaves (seafood dishes). Banana leaves can sometimes be found at Asian markets in the frozen food aisle, and at Latino markets, where they are called *hojas de plátano*.

THICKENING SOUPS AND SAUCES

Cornstarch is used to thicken soups and sauces. Mix one part cornstarch to two parts water and mix into a paste. Be sure to sieve the cornstarch before use. At the end of the cooking process, an egg yolk can be added, if desired. Remove from heat, otherwise the egg will curdle. The same applies to agar agar and condensed milk.

FISH

Before adding any fish to a dish, rub it all over with salt and lemon. Let it stand *for a while*, then rinse the fish with cold water, and dry well with a clean towel. Are you deep-frying the fish? Add a piece of turmeric root to the oil when frying raw fish to absorb any unpleasant smells.

VEGETABLES

When making *sajur* (wet vegetable dishes), frozen vegetables are acceptable if certain fresh ones are not available. Avoid using canned vegetables, as these are often too soft. The best sajurs are those where the vegetables are still somewhat crisp; the vitamins are retained and the taste is better. Add softer vegetables to the pan five minutes before serving *just to heat through*.

INGREDIENTS, HERBS & SPICES

INGREDIENTS, HERBS & SPICES

A good Indo Dutch household is prepared to expect the unexpected. That means a fully stocked pantry and being able to whip up a tasty meal in no time. In this chapter, I will be describing various ingredients, herbs and spices. Many Indo Dutch dishes have actually derived their unique flavors specifically from substitute or dried ingredients. These days, most herbs and spices are available fresh. Many spice mixtures (*bumbu*) are even available ready-made. These are convenient time-savers but making your own tastes best of course. I have chosen the modern spelling for the names of the ingredients, and how they are known in the English language. For the names of dishes I have opted to stay faithful to the old Indo Dutch spelling. When you see 'oe' that is the old spelling for 'u' and is pronounced as 'oo' in 'boo'. Sometimes you will see 'c' or 'tj' in names, which is pronounced as 'ch' in 'check'.

"Everyone has their own 'hand of cooking.' It is difficult to capture in measurements."

—*Oma*

A LITTLE OF THIS, A LITTLE OF THAT

Indo Dutch cooking is different from Western cooking. The cooks are hailed for their resourcefulness and intuitive approach. In Western cooking, the recipes provide a safe structure as they are usually followed precisely and ingredients are measured carefully. Indo Dutch cuisine is more casual. Although this offers more flexibility

and the recipes tend to be more forgiving, it is still a challenge to feel comfortable with this style of cooking. In this book I provide quantities, weights and measurements that you can use as a starting point on your voyage of discovery. The secret to delectable fare lies in uncovering the precise balance of fragrances and the five basic tastes: sweet, sour, salt, bitter, and umami. Sometimes you may discover that a dish tastes even better when it has just a hint of sweetness. In Indo Dutch cuisine, you learn to cook by watching, by tasting and helping in the kitchen. If this is not your background, then you simply begin by learning the basics and sticking to the recommended measurements. A recipe is a guideline. When you eventually develop your own personal taste, do not hesitate to bend the rules. Because the intensity of the flavor of an ingredient can vary from day to day and everyone has his or her own preferences, only your tongue can tell you how much more of something you should add. If you do not like a particular ingredient, just leave it out - simple as that!

THE DIFFERENCE BETWEEN HERBS AND SPICES

In this section I will provide a short description of the terms for the seasonings used in numerous Indo Dutch dishes, which are sometimes used interchangeably.

Herbs are the leaves—and sometimes also the flowers—of plants that grow in Europe, North America and subtropical regions. Parsley, celery, thyme, rosemary, oregano and basil are all well-known herbs.

Coriander/cilantro and mint are herbs as well. When the fresh variety is used, they have a more intense, aromatic fragrance. Many herbs can be grown at home on a windowsill or in the garden.

Spices is the collective term for several aromatic, dried parts of a plant, usually from tropical regions, for instance the seeds (mustard, coriander), buds (cloves) and sometimes the stamens (saffron). It also includes the fruit (peppercorn), root (various types of ginger) and bark (cinnamon). Other spices are nutmeg, cumin, cardamom and curry (a blend of spices). Ground spices are often more fragrant and are have a more intense flavor. They are available for purchase in small quantities; however, it is best to grind your own.

Note: grinding herbs and spices in a food processor will produce less flavor and fragrance than when you crush or mash them with a mortar and pestle. Bear in mind that a little liquid should be added to keep the blades moving smoothly during the grinding process. This can be oil if the *bumbu* is being fried, or coconut milk, stock or water if it is for simmering.

SEQUENCE OF USING HERBS AND SPICES

Begin by finely chopping onions, shallots and garlic and set aside. Follow with the hard, dried spices and nuts, and tough, fibrous rhizomes such as galangal (laos, lengkuas) and lemongrass (sereh). You can use the mortar and pestle to crush or bruise ginger root (jahe) and lemongrass, or you can add them to the pan in one piece (twist the stalk of the lemongrass into a knot). After this, add the softer roots, such as peeled and sliced ginger, turmeric (kunyit/curcuma), kaempferia galanga (kencur, aromatic or sand ginger) and fresh or dried chilis (cabe). Finely slice leafy herbs such as daun salam (Indonesian bay leaves) and jeruk purut (kaffir lime) before finely slicing or crushing them with the mortar and pestle; you could also add these to the dish intact.

After everything has been crushed well, continue with the juicier ingredients such as chopped shallots and garlic. Finally, add shrimp paste, tamarind juice or other juices, and blend everything together well.

Fry or simmer this *bumbu* according to the recipe. If it is being fried, heat a small amount of oil over low to medium heat, then sauté the *bumbu* until it begins to smell fragrant; this will take about two to three minutes. Sometimes, small chunks of meat or poultry will be added. Keep sautéing until the *bumbu* coats the meat and has changed color.

Ingredients

Indo Dutch cuisine has numerous ingredients to call its own. Below I will describe those most essential to the recipes in this book. Some ingredients can only be found in Chinese and Southeast Asian supermarkets. At the end I provide a list of substitutes for hard to source ingredients.

COCONUT MILK (**Santan**) Also known as *klapper* milk. Used to enhance the flavor in dishes, including desserts and beverages. Not to be confused with coconut water. Coconut milk is made by mixing grated coconut flesh with water and squeezing it to extract the juice. Creamed coconut or coconut cream concentrate is the thicker, condensed variety. Add tepid water to make coconut milk. A block of *santan* (concentrated coconut milk = creamed coconut, dilute 7 ounces with water makes about 4 cups coconut milk or 2 tablespoons coconut and mix 10 tablespoons water) is a convenient alternative to canned coconut milk because you don't have to open a whole can if you only want a small amount. It can be added right into the pan as is towards the end. Coconut milk is also available canned. Instant coconut ground is the best substitute for fresh coconut milk. To prepare, follow the instructions on the package. **Condensed, sweetened coconut**, with its rich and creamy texture, is suitable for desserts and pastries. Coconut milk has many things in common with milk, such as color, curdling and spoiling. *Santan* can curdle quickly when heated or when using acidic ingredients (e.g. *asam* water, lemon juice, vinegar). Do not cook a dish with *santan* too long, and add the acidic ingredient slowly while stirring well. Coconut milk

can be frozen. The creamed coconut block I recommend is 'Let's Do Organic Creamed Coconut' (take 2 tablespoons coconut and mix with 10 tablespoons water). My favorite canned coconut milk is Mae Ploy imported from Thailand. **Fresh grated or desiccated** (dried, finely grated) coconut unsweetened – used to make crisp spiced coconut for serundeng or urap urap.

CHILIES, BIRD'S EYE (Lombok, Cabe Rawit) The Indonesian name for Spanish pepper, chili pepper and lombok are often used interchangeably in The Netherlands. Fresh chili peppers come in different sizes and the amount of heat increases as the size of the chili pepper diminishes. In Indonesia, the red (ripe) chili pepper is called *cabe merah*, the green chili pepper is called *cabe hijau*, and the small, extremely spicy bird's eye is *cabe rawit*. A smaller (dried) type can also be called *rawit*. They are approximately ½ - 1 inch long, and are hotter than larger peppers. The pepper is chopped finely, or crushed with a mortar and pestle. To reduce the spiciness/heat of a dish, first slice the pepper lengthwise, then scrape out the seeds and ribs.

Instead of fresh *lombok*, 1 tablespoon of *sambal* can be substituted. If you prefer a milder dish, replace the *lombok* with a red bell pepper. Remove the seeds from a bell pepper also.

RAW CHILI PASTE (Sambal Oelek) Added to a dish as a condiment (seasoning) or as the base for making other sambals; made of ground chili peppers. Used raw, or cooked with the addition of onion, *terasi*, sugar, spices, etc.

CHILI SAUCE Bottled chili sauce and used like ketchup to accompany the meal. Different brands offer different kinds and range in hotness and sweetness.

SHALLOTS (Bawang Mera) Type of (Javanese) onion. The red variety is used for chicken, meat and fish dishes, or chopped or ground into *bumbus*. The white variety is used in vegetable pickles (*atjar*), and also deep-fried to use as a garnish (*bawang merah goreng*) for soto, sate, gado gado etc. Shallots have a richer aroma

and taste sweeter. Slice them thinly before pounding. Shallots can be substituted by double the amount of onions.

GARLIC (Bawang Putih) Like shallot and onion, is a member of the allium family. Pounded, grated or sliced thinly.

PALM SUGAR (Gula Java) Javanese sugar derived from the juice of the palm tree, which is condensed and thickened into liquid sugar. Available in light to dark brown varieties. When crystallized into blocks, it can be grated or melted in the microwave. Store tightly sealed in a cool, dry location to prevent drying up. A substitute is brown sugar or superfine/caster sugar.

TAMARIND (Asam) The pulp of this soft fruit lends a slight sourness to dishes. It is used to balance out the flavors of sauces and salads and to tenderize meat and poultry. It is available as a ready-made paste or in blocks (compressed fruit pulp without the fibers and seeds removed). To make *asam* water, rub one part of this pulp between the fingers and thumb, and dissolve in two parts water, then sieve.

KAFFIR LIME (Jeruk Limau) The juice of this small, yellow or dark green citrus fruit (smaller than a golf ball) has a sour flavor, ideal for the preparation of sambals, and such. To give a dish a strong lemon flavor, the rind of the *jeruk limo* (also called *jeruk purut* in Indonesia) can be added while cooking or steaming. In The Netherlands, *jeruk limo* is fairly easily available. If the fruit itself cannot be found, the juice of a larger lime or that of a lemon can be used.

FERMENTED SHRIMP PASTE (Terasi) Also called *belacan*. Used to add savory, umami quality to dishes. Mashed and sun-dried fermented shrimp, compressed into blocks. Notable for its pungent scent and unambiguous flavor. The smell fades when roasted; *terasi* is usually sold pre-roasted (labeled as *terasi bakar*). *Terasi* is a seasoning in many Indo Dutch recipes, for example, it is delicious in *sambal*. The fermentation process produces the penetrating scent. When used in moderation (according to the recipe), the strong flavor dissipates, but leaves behind a distinctive aroma. Store *terasi* at room temperature in an airtight container. If you have fresh *terasi*, roast it over a flame first, or in the oven wrapped in aluminum foil (to curb the smell), then crumble and add to your dish. *Terasi* can also be diluted with tepid water; the water is then added to your dish. The color of *terasi* varies from purplish pink to brownish black.

SMALL DRIED SHRIMPS These dried shrimps are salty, mildly fishy and they are dense, meaty and potent. Good for soups or nasi goreng.

BLACK SHRIMP PASTE (Petis udang) A syrupy dark paste made of cooked shrimps. Used for example as a dressing for *rudjak* – a fruit salad or in the sauce for saté kambing.

SOY SAUCE (Ketjap) Condiment made from soybeans. Available in three types: sweet (*manis*), semi-sweet (*sedang*) and salty (*asin*). Thick, syrupy *ketjap manis* is the most common type used in Indo Dutch cuisine. *Ketjap* is usually added while cooking, but can also be used at the end. *Ketjap asin* is often used as a salt-substitute. If *manis* is not available, you can use Chinese soy sauce with the addition of brown sugar or molasses. I recommend Kecap by Conimex.

MAGGI SAUCE A pungent seasoning sauce originally from Switzerland but is used in many Asian dishes. Just a few drops can give you that delicious savory (umami) taste. Used like soy sauce, in soups, noodles, stir-fries etc.

SOYBEAN PASTE (Tauco/Tauchu Sauce) A thick golden brown condiment made of fermented soybeans and originally from China – vegetarian. Tauchu has a distinctive, slightly wine-like flavor. It is used both in Indonesia, as well as Chinese cuisine. Used as tastemaker in stir-fry dishes and also in sambal. Kwong Hung Seng Sauce (Yellow Bean Sauce) - 19fl Oz (Pack of 1) (no MSG) – from Dragonfly. Tao jiao from Healthy Boy Brand (contains MSG).

FERMENTED SOYBEAN (Tempeh) Made from whole cooked soybeans to which yeast has been added. A firm cake is produced through the process of fermentation (fungus). Unlike tofu, which is made of soymilk. Tempeh is richer in protein, fiber, vitamins and minerals. Tempeh has a mildly nutty flavor and originated in Indonesia. It is available in flat, plastic-wrapped cakes. Can be cooked, marinated, fried or steamed. Can be frozen for longer-term storage if protected with plastic wrap. Note that tempeh is prone to spoil, as the fungus will continue fermenting if left out at room temperature.

SOYBEAN CURD (Tahu/Tofu) Derived from soybeans (soybean curd), and due to its high protein content, an excellent meat replacement. Available in blocks, and keeps well for a few days when immersed in water and refrigerated. To prepare soft tofu: press for 15 minutes before cooking to remove liquid; pat dry with paper towel. Firm tofu has been pressed further; it can easily be sliced to add to stews or stir- fried dishes, or grilled or deep-fried. The spongy, fried cubes absorb a lot of moisture when added to dishes.

EGG NOODLES (Mie Telor) Pasta made from wheat flour, eggs and water. Boil the noodles in plenty of water; cooking time varies. Run cold water over the cooked noodles in a colander to prevent sticking. Loosen the *mie* with a fork, stir in 1 teaspoon of oil, and set aside for use later.

RICE VERMICELLI (Bihun) Very thin Chinese noodles made of rice flour, also known as *mihun*. There are various types, such as thin strands, or wide and flat "sticks". *Bihun* originally comes from Southeast Asia, where it is used as the base for stir-fry dishes and in soups. Rice noodles are low in fat and calories, and therefore a healthy part of a meal. Not to be confused with *suun* (cellophane noodles made from mung bean starch).

MUNG BEAN NOODLES (Suun/Sohun) Translucent, glossy vermicelli, also called glass noodles, cellophane noodles, *laksa* or Chinese vermicelli. Made of ground mung beans (*katjang idjo*), the basis of bean sprouts (*taugé*) and are gluten free! Unsoaked *suun* can be added directly to soup (*soto*), or when warmed, to stir-fry and vegetable dishes, and as a filling for savory pastries (*pastel*). The unsoaked noodles can also be deep-fried and will puff up, to create crunchy *krupuk*-like strands. When *suun* is cooked, it can become tough and jelly-like; it is better to simply pour some warm water or boiling stock over it.

RICE (Beras - uncooked & Nasi - cooked) The rice most eaten in Indonesia, the Netherlands and North America is long-grain. In my family we prefer jasmine because it is fluffy, separates better and is well known for its mild floral aroma – hence the name jasmine. Short-grain rice is stickier and starchier.

STICKY RICE (**Ketan**) also known as glutinous rice (in the sense of being glue-like, does not contain gluten), has a high starch content and is used for example for lemper ayam and bubur.

COMPRESSED RICE CAKES (**Lontong**) Compressed rice is prepared in cylindrical shaped banana leaves or plastic perforated bags. Lontong is best served cold and often paired with stews and peanut sauce. When buying rice look for the imported kinds from Thailand widely available at Chinese or Southeast Asian markets.

IDAHO RUSSET POTATOES (**Kentang**) Used for mash like Dutch potato-kale mash (boerenkool) and Dutch fries. You can also use Yukon Gold potatoes.

CASSAVA (**Ketela Pohon**) Also known as *ubi pohon* or *singkong*. Tuberous root of the shrub-like cassava plant, native to South America. Eaten as a substitute for potatoes and rice; also deep-fried for snack crackers (*kripik singkong*). Cassava is ground into tapioca flour (tepung, and can be used as a thickening agent, just like cornstarch. A well-known dish is *ketela rambat* (sweet potato)

MUNG BEAN FLOUR (**Tepung Hun Kwe**) Flour made from mung beans (*kacang ijo*), the small, green beans more commonly known as the unsprouted form of bean sprouts (*tauge*). Mung bean flour is the main ingredient in cellophane/glass noodles and the broader/thicker "starch noodles", and is what the jelly-like slivers in the beverage *cendol/tjendol* are made of. Also used in other Indonesian confections and is a component of pastries (kwe lapis). Preferred in desserts over rice flour for a better texture. Gluten free!

RICE FLOUR (**Tepung Beras**) This flour is made of ground rice and often used in desserts and part of a deep frying batter (like pisang goreng and frikadel djagoeng)

GLUTINOUS RICE FLOUR (**Tepung Ketan**) Made from glutinous rice and used mostly for desserts (like klepon). Gluten free.

TAPIOCA FLOUR (**Tepung Tapioka**) Cassava is ground into tapioca flour and can be used as a thickening agent, just like cornstarch. Gluten free.

Herbs & Spices

GALANGAL (**Laos**) The rhizome of the greater galangal plant, also called *lengkuas*. Fresh (young) galangal root has a warm, herbal, light ginger flavor, with a hint of cinnamon, and emits a refreshing fragrance. When used fresh, peel the root and shred with a grater or slice. *Laos* can also be purchased as dried slices, ground or frozen. As a substitute for fresh *laos*, soak the dried slices in boiling water for 30 minutes before using in *sajoers or sotos*, or when using ground, use 1 teaspoon for ½ inch fresh root. 1½ tablespoons of fresh, grated *laos* root equals approximately 1 teaspoon ground.

LESSER GALANGAL (**Kencur/Aromatic Ginger**) Belongs to the ginger family. The thick root stems are used as a seasoning. Available fresh, ground, or sliced and dried. Its flavor can quickly overpower a dish, so use sparingly.

GINGER (**Jahe**) The root of the ginger plant. Can be peeled, bruised, grated, or sliced, and is also available ground. Try to always use fresh, light brown ginger root for the herb mixture. Ginger has the tendency to enhance the flavor of other ingredients. When buying fresh ginger root, pay attention that it is not shriveled or hard, or has mold on the ends, otherwise it will be dry and tough. Look for tender, fresh roots with pale pink shoots or buds. Never deep-fry ginger root, as it will get bitter.

TURMERIC (Kunyit) Also known as *kunir*, this is the rhizome/root of the Indian turmeric plant, most often found in ground form. Belongs to the ginger family, and is one of the main components of curry ground. In Indonesia, turmeric is predominantly used to add a yellow tint to white rice. This yellow rice (*nasi kuning*) is eaten at special occasions. The thin outer peel of the *kunyit* root is removed, then added to the rice during cooking, after which it is removed before serving. Can be found fresh (purchase a darker root), frozen or ground.

TURMERIC LEAF (Daun kunyit) This leaf is long and wide and used fresh or dried in West Sumatran dishes like rendang (beef in coconut milk) kalio, gulai etc.

LEMONGRASS (Daun Sereh) A fragrant herb that emits a citrus-like aroma, similar to citronella grass and lime grass. Added to dishes and marinades to brighten and enrich the flavor. Available fresh, frozen, dried and ground. The slender ends of the young stalks are also suitable for using as skewers, which adds an extra layer of flavor. Slice the ends of the stalks at a sharp angle and thread the meat evenly onto the skewers.

SALAM LEAF (Daun Salam) Used the same way as bay/laurel leaves in Western cuisine. Bruised, then added to the pan to simmer with the other ingredients, it lends an unmistakable flavor to various types of stews. Do not use bay/laurel leaves as a substitute, as these have a different flavor. Salam is available fresh, frozen or dried.

KAFFIR LIME LEAF (Daun Jeruk Purut) Doubled/connected leaves of the kaffir lime; imparts a mellow, fruity citrus flavor to dishes - available dried or fresh.

PETIS

ASAM

TERASI

PANDAN LEAF (Daun Pandan) In Southeast Asia, pandan leaves are as common as vanilla is in Western countries. They give a unique taste, special aroma and visual appeal to desserts and drinks. They are also used in some savory dishes and added to rice while it is boiling. Knot the leaves and bruise them before adding to the pan. Available fresh or dried, and can also be found as bottled extract.

BASIL LEAF (Daun Kemangi) Also known as Indonesian basil. The lemon-scented leaves are added to a dish at the last moment to enhance the flavor of fish, poultry and meat, and are also used as a garnish. There is also *daun selasih*, which is similar to European basil. Store fresh basil in a cool, dark place (45-60 °F). Do not store in the fridge, as this will cause the leaves to blacken and the flavor to fade. Purchase fresh plants with sturdy stems and bright leaves without discoloration. Wash the leaves shortly before use, and simmer in the food to boost its flavor even further.

CHIVES (Daun Kucai) This Chinese version has a finer leaf than the Western version. Finely cut, used as garnish for stir-fried dishes or soto.

LEEK & SPRING ONION (Prei, Daun Bawang) Leek has flat green leaves and the spring onion has hollow, tube-like leaves. Use only the white and light green portion.

CORIANDER (Ketumbar) The seeds of a bushy plant, native to Southern Europe. Can be found both as dried seeds or ground, and is often used in combination with *jintan*. Coriander leaves - cilantro or Indonesian parsley - are also used, both as an ingredient as well as a garnish. However, coriander leaves have a much brighter scent than parsley: it is more intense and the flavor lingers. *Ketumbar* and *jintan* are used in a two-to-one ratio: for each indicated amount of *ketumbar*, use half that of *jintan*.

CANDLENUT (Kemiri) Intensely flavored, creamy nut from the candlenut tree, resembling macadamia nuts. They are favored for lending a creamy texture to sauces. Candlenuts are purchased pre-shelled and roasted or baked. Before use, toast the nuts in an oil-

KETJAP MANIS

GULA DJAWA

SAMBAL OELEK

free sauté pan or wok over medium-high heat, turning regularly until they turn slightly brown. Then pulverize them and cook with other seasonings. Due to their high oil content, they are quick to spoil and turn rancid; keep them in a tightly covered container in the refrigerator. Candlenuts can be grated with a nutmeg grater or crushed with the *cobek* and *ulekan (pestle and mortar)*.

CANARIUM NUT (Kenari) A sweet Java almond that can be eaten raw.

CARDAMOM (Kapulaga) Fragrant black seeds bring flavor to soups, sauces and commonly used in spekkoek.

CUMIN (Jintan) Available as seeds and ground. Often used in recipes together with *ketumbar* (coriander). Can be somewhat overpowering, so use in moderation.

CLOVES (Cengkeh) Nail-shaped spice, in whole or ground form. 1 tablespoon cloves = 1 teaspoon ground cloves.

NUTMEG (Pala) Sold whole and in ground form.

CINNAMON (Kayu Manis) Use dried bark whole or use ground.

ANISEED (Adas Manis) Used in dishes cooked with coconut milk (gulai) or curry.

PEPPER (Merica) Both black and white peppercorns are crushed just before use.

STAR ANISE (Bunga Kawak): shaped like an eight-pointed star. Often used in Chinese or Indian dishes and certain regions in Indonesia

KLUWEK NUT (Kluak/Kluwak) A hard, oily black nut with an extremely dominant flavor. Used to color or season meat-based dishes. Crack the nut, remove the seed and chop it finely or crush it, then mix with water. Used to prepare *rawon*, for example. Not easily found outside of Indonesia.

CURRY (Kari) Curry originated in India. *Kari* means sauce; it was adopted by the British, and changed to 'curry'. It is a blend of various ground spices; the combination varies by region. In most cases, it contains the following: ginger (*jahe*), cardamom, cumin (*jintan*), coriander (*ketumbar*), cloves (*cengkeh*), turmeric (*kunjit*) for a vivid yellow color, and black pepper. Used in dishes such as *gulai kambing*, *rendang* and *ajam por*. The Javanese name for curry is '*opor*', and on Sumatra it is called '*gulai*' with the addition of cinnamon. Available ground or as a paste.

SPICES MIXTURE (Bumbu/Boemboe) Blend of herbs and spices, traditionally crushed in a mortar; the foundation of many Indo Dutch recipes. Mixing herbs and spices with oil makes this paste. Most *bumbu* mixtures are available pre-made and perfectly portioned, but making your own seasoning tastes best of course. General tip: Begin by *oelek*-ing (crushing) the *bumbu* prior to preparing the other ingredients for cooking, such as the vegetables, meat, fish and poultry. This will facilitate finishing each dish one after the other. Shelf-stable condiments such as sambal, vegetable pickles and *krupuk* can be set out on the table ahead of time.

Fruits, Buds & Leaves

EGGPLANT (Terung) also known as aubergines come in several varieties: long violet, and small round green, can be cooked and mostly eaten as a salad.

BITTER GOURD (Pare) bright green colored bitter gourd. Reduce bitterness by rubbing salt to sliced pieces and squeezing until tender.

YOUNG JACKFRUIT (Nangka Muda) unripe jackfruit with small seeds and firm flesh can be used in vegetable dishes (in coconut milk).

BANANA (**Pisang**) Baked in butter or deep fried in a batter.

PUMPKIN (**Labu Kuning**) Used in a dessert dish with coconut milk called kolak

JACKFRUIT (**Nangka**) One of the largest fruits in the world. The sweet flesh lies in sections inside a bumpy, yellow-brown skin. In Indonesia, jackfruit is consumed raw, cooked as part of a dish, and sometimes fried. Its large brown seeds can also be roasted and eaten like nuts. Jackfruit is also available canned.

CHAYOTTE (**Labu Siam**) Unripe chayottes are boiled and used in a salad.

BAMBOO SHOOTS (**Rebung**) The young shoots - or sprouts - of the bamboo plant, which are harvested as soon as they appear above ground. Only available canned in Western countries. They have a mild flavor and are used in Indonesian, but especially Chinese, cuisine.

YAM BEAN (**Bengkuang**) This is known in the US as jicama. Used in salads or pickles.

RADISH (**Lobak**) Chinese root also known as Japanese daikon radish, often used in salads and pickles.

BEAN SPROUTS (**Taugé**) A day-old sprout from green beans or soybeans, with a shorter and harder stem. It is used in a salad, like Gado Gado. A two-day old sprout is longer and can have a brownish tail, which must be removed. I had to do that many times when I was growing up.

CILANTRO (**Daun Ketumbar**) Fresh leaves related to the parsley family with a distinctly different smell and a much stronger flavor. A popular ingredient in Asian, Middle Eastern and Latin American cuisines.

ITALIAN PARSLEY (**Seledri/Selderij**) Flat-leaf parsley, featuring broad, serrated leaves.

CURLY PARSLEY Has a grassy flavor and decorative ruffled leaves, perfect for garnish.

STAR FRUIT (**Belimbing, Carambola**) Yellowish-green star-shaped fruit with a sweet-tart flavor. The juice of this fruit is used in cold beverages. It is often sliced and added to fruit salads or used to garnish cocktails.

DURIAN Also known as "stinky fruit" due to its pungent smell. The flavor and scent is incomparable. This large fruit has yellowish-white, creamy pulp and a spiky peel.

WATER SPINACH (**Bayam air**) Asian leafy green plant, also known as swamp cabbage or water spinach with a pleasant, crisp, hollow stem and long, green leaves. Often used in stir-fry dishes. In the past, was substituted with spinach but is now available in the US. Remove the hard stems and the older leaves, as they have a bitter taste.

GARTER BEAN/CHINESE LONG BEAN (**Kacang Pandjang**) Resembles long string beans, although the flavor is somewhat more intense. For many years, green beans were used as a substitute, measures about 10 - 12 inches long. *Katjang pandjang* should be cleaned the same way as green beans, and cut to size before use.

STINK BEAN (**Peteh**) Bean with a pungent smell. Available fresh or frozen; also pickled or dried in jars. They are often used in the preparation of *sambals* and *sajurs*.

PEANUTS (**Kacang**). Used to make sauces. When bought raw, buy de-shelled and dry roast them in a wok or skillet over moderate heat for 10-15 minutes, stirring often until they start to color. Alternatively, use crunchy unsalted peanut butter as a wonderful time saver.

KEMIRI   KLUWAK   PETEH

VEGETARIAN CRACKERS (**Emping Belindju/Melindju**) Also known as vegetarian *krupuk*. The kernel of the fruit is cooked, flattened and dried in the sun. Then the dried chips are fried in oil, causing them to swell. Drain in a colander, dry on paper towels and sprinkle with salt before serving.

SHRIMP CRACKERS (**Kroepoek/Krupuk Udang**) Sun-dried crackers made from puréed shrimp and sago, tapioca or rice flour. When deep-fried, swells up and becomes crispy and light in the hot oil.

ROSE SYRUP Fragrant syrup (sugar water) made of rose petals. Used in desserts and drinks.

SWEETENED CONDENSED MILK (Susu Manis): Made from cow's milk from which the water has been removed and to which sugar has been added. Often used in desserts and as sweeteners in hot coffee or iced beverages like stroop susu.

Wrappers

FLOUR WRAPPERS Come in different sizes and are used for egg rolls (loempia), size 9" x 9", or smaller for fried wontons (pangsit goreng) or steamed wontons (siomay), size 3½" x 3½". They are available in the freezer section of Chinese and Southeast Asian supermarkets.

BANANA LEAF (**Daun Pisang**) Leaves of the banana plant are natural wrappers and used to enclose food. They give flavor and aroma to steamed and grilled dishes.

Available frozen. Before use, cut the leaf to size, wash well and dry with a tea towel. To soften the leaf and make it supple, pour warm water over it and dry again. You could also hold the leaf over a gas flame or place briefly in the broiler. The leaf will become pliable, which will prevent it from tearing during wrapping. Next, lay the ingredients of the dish in the center in a cylindrical shape. Fold the leaf around the filling and secure the ends with toothpicks. The packet is then cooked or steamed on both sides over a charcoal flame.

Oil

COOKING For high-heat applications, like deep-frying, I recommend peanut oil. Other suitable oils with a high smoking point are: corn, canola and sunflower oil. Coconut oil has a lower smoking point and offers a unique, bold flavor, which can taste a little overbearing.

SESAME OIL Primarily used as a seasoning for its nutty flavor and is usually added to the food after cooking due to its low smoking point.

Substitutes

The yearning for the taste of home, and lack of availability of authentic ingredients, prompted the search for alternative ingredients in the former Dutch East Indies, and later, in The Netherlands and other migratory countries. This is how Indo Dutch fusion cuisine was conceived and evolved: out of necessity, combining local ingredients as a substitute for those that were lacking. Fresh spices from Indonesia were not available, but dried or ground seasonings were.

These days, much is available fresh. This once again affects the distinctive flavor of Indo Dutch cuisine. In the beginning, my Oma used substitutes or dried herbs (e.g. *pandan* and *salam* leaves) and spices, usually ground (such as ginger, *kunyit, kencur, jintan* and *sereh*) in her restaurant. Some ingredients were not available in The Netherlands for a long time, and sometimes not at all. Before that,

replacements or substitutes were used, which somewhat resembled the original ingredients in terms of taste, or were close enough. The use of substitutes in particular is what caused certain dishes to taste completely different in The Netherlands than in the Dutch East Indies. In this way, the Indonesian vegetables that are featured in the recipes can be replaced by American vegetable varieties.

See below a list of potential substitutes for different Southeast Asian ingredients:

AGAR AGAR - gelatin sheets or powdered gelatin

ASAM WATER - vinegar, lemon juice

BLIMBING - rhubarb

COCONUT MILK - desiccated unsweetened coconut soaked in water/milk, or regular milk with a little sugar added

CHILI PEPPER - Jalapenos, for less heat go for the big banana peppers – mild

DAUN KEMANGI - basil / baby celery leaves

DAUN PISANG – aluminum foil, plastic wrap

DAUN SALAM - curry leaves (not bay leaves)

DJERUK PURUT - lemon juice, grated lemon rind

GALANGAL -ginger or ginger paste

GULA JAWA -brown sugar or maple syrup, molasses

IKAN ASIN -pickled herring, salt cod

KAFFIR LIME - Lime zest

KANGKUNG (aquatic plants) - curly endive, spinach, turnip greens, purslane/pigweed (do not overcook).

KATJANG PANDJANG - string beans or green beans (haricots verts)

KEMANGI - basil

KEMIRI - macadamia nuts or raw cashew or almond

KETJAP ASIN - Maggi seasoning, or Chinese/Japanese soy sauce

KETJAP MANIS - Maggi seasoning or Chinese/Japanese soy sauce with brown sugar or molasses added

KLUWEK – no substitute

LAOS – In case fresh is not available, dried laos root is available in Southeast Asian supermarkets

LOMBOK - sambal oelek (jar), ground piri piri/cayenne pepper

MIE - vermicelli, angel hair pasta

PALM SUGAR – brown sugar or maple syrup, molasses

REBUNG - rutabaga

SEREH - grated lemon rind

SHALLOTS - red or Spanish onions, or twice the number of regular *Bombay* onions

TERASI – Belacan (Malay), Bagoong (Filipino) Kapi (Thai), anchovy paste, fish stock cube. For vegan dish use yellow soybean paste or yellow miso.

DJAHE   LAOS   KUNYIT

THE FAMILY RECIPES

I remember that the potluck parties, where family and friends would gather, were looked forward to with great anticipation. At these events, it was customary for guests to bring along something tasty from their own kitchen. It would not be uncommon for people to try to one-up each other and subtly lure everyone's attention to his or her specialty/culinary contribution. After all, who doesn't like compliments? It soon became competitive. Among the many compliments to each other, like "enak (delicious), wonderful, guri (full-flavored) to heavenly,"; you would also hear the murmurs from a sullen cook whose efforts hadn't received the desired recognition. A competitor's dish was disparaged with such remarks as "Kurang asin (not enough salt)!" "My mother makes it better!" or "That's not how you make this!" doubtless accompanied by a big wink. If you asked the master chef, "Oh, just how did you make this?" they would get very secretive. With much effort (coaxing and cajoling), I would sometimes be able to tease out the recipe. Once at home, I would set to work in my laboratory, with ample fuss and heady fumes. Unfortunately, the results never quite tasted the same.

This was possibly because "one's own touch" is different than that of the chef's; or perhaps because—no doubt purposely—an important ingredient was omitted by the creator. And this is how Auntie Rora's pisang goreng, Uncle Donald's tahoe telor petis and Aunt Lenie's pastei remained a closely guarded secret. Of course they did this to make you return to them. Luckily for us, my oma and mother were not so tough. In this chapter you will find my personal selection of favorite secret recipes, many of which are passed on by my oma and mother.

RICE, NOODLES, POTATOES & BREAD

RICE

Cooking rice is an art: not the parboiled or pre-cooked kind, but simply the traditional technique of cooking beras *(uncooked white rice) in a steamer or electric rice cooker.* Putih *means white; there are several varieties of rice. We often use jasmine rice (also known as aromatic Thai rice or pandan rice). This variety is long-grained with a subtle nutty scent and a pandan-like, gentle, full flavor. White rice can be prepared in various ways: in a pan, a steamer on the stove, or in an electric rice cooker, which is the fastest and easiest. If you cook it in a pan, make sure that it does not boil dry or end up being served as porridge. The rice should have a tender grain, but not be too sticky.*

NASI POETIH

WHITE RICE

Wash the uncooked rice (*beras*): place it in the pan, add water and swirl it around with your hand. Remove any rocks or dirt you might find. Pour off the water and add fresh. Repeat this process two more times until the water is clear. Well-cleaned rice tastes better, is less sticky and has a lovely sheen.

COOKING

Using a rice cooker: close the lid and press the start button.

Using two pans: Use one pan to boil the rice on the stove without a lid. At the same time, boil another, larger pan to steam the rice. This type of steamer is also called a *kukusan*, an enamel pan with matching colander and lid, or more traditionally, a cone-shaped steam basket made of woven bamboo. If you use a separate colander, make sure it does not touch the water. Use a well-closing lid. Pan 1: Bring the water and rice to a boil. Wait until the water has been absorbed into the rice, and small holes can be seen over the entire surface. Transfer the rice to the colander. Cover with the lid, and steam the rice over high heat, folding occasionally. When the rice is done, keep it warm over a low flame until you are ready to serve. If necessary, add more water to the steamer (bottom pan).

No separate steamer: Bring the rice to a boil, uncovered. Turn the heat down to the lowest setting, replace the lid, then simmer gently for about 20 minutes until done. Remove from heat, leaving the lid in place, and allow to rest for 10 minutes. Before serving, fluff the rice gently with a fork.

Tip: Account for one cup of rice per person. After washing, put the rice in the pan and add the correct amount of water. The ratio is 1:1½, this means one cup of rice to a cup and a half of water. An easy method is to add water to the pan with rice until it reaches the first joint of your index finger above the rice.

NASI KOENING

YELLOW RICE

This fragrant rice dish is made with coconut milk and ground turmeric, which gives it its yellow tint. The rice is often served cone-shaped on a flat wicker basket covered with a banana leaf, surrounded by a variety of dry dishes. A platter such as this, also known as Tumpeng, is often served - in accordance with traditional Javanese custom - at special, ceremonial occasions, called a selamatan. The selamatan is an occurrence of religious or social importance, such as a birth, wedding, new home, the day of a funeral, and the fortieth day after a death. It is a ceremony of giving thanks and to ask for the blessings and favors of the gods. Selamatan is celebrated with family and neighbors. When this dish is prepared without ground turmeric, it is called nasi gurih.

Note: This dish is usually prepared for a celebration meal, where many people are served at a time. This recipe is enough for 10-15 people, with a minimum of ½ cup rice per person.

Soak the rice and ketan in water with one teaspoon ground turmeric and the lemon juice for a couple of hours, then rinse it with fresh water. Simmer the coconut milk with the pandan leaf, sereh, laos, djeruk purut, and remaining kunjit. Steam the rice until halfway done then transfer it to the warm coconut milk to soak. After 30 minutes, steam the rice again until fully cooked.

Tip: Scoop the rice onto a large platter and garnish with the bawang goreng (fried onions), sambal, tempeh kering, and omelet.

4 cups rice
2 cups ketan (sticky rice)
2 teaspoons kunjit (ground turmeric), divided
1 tablespoon lemon juice
2 cups santan (coconut milk)
3 daun djeruk purut (kaffir lime leaves)
1 pandan leaf, in thirds
1 stalk sereh (lemongrass) (use the bottom 2 inches)
1 piece laos (galanga, 1 inch thick, 1 knuckle-length)
Garnish:
Bawang goreng (fried onions)
Sambal
Tempeh Kering (fermented soybean cake)
thinly sliced omelet

NASI GORENG WITH TJEPLOK

FRIED RICE WITH FRIED EGG

This one-pot meal originated from frying up the previous day's leftovers. In Indonesia, nasi goreng is often eaten as a breakfast dish. The word 'tjeplok' refers to a fried egg and as is common in Indonesian language, a name given to mimic the sound (onomatopoeia) of an egg landing in the pan.

Cut the corned beef or other meat into small cubes and set aside. Heat the oil in a wok and sauté the onion and garlic until translucent. Return the meat to the pan, along with the leeks and celery onions, and cook until the mixture looks somewhat dry. Add the diluted terasi, stock cube, sambal, ketjap and rice. Add the dry, cooked rice (preferably from the day before), and continue scooping until everything is mixed together well.

Stir-fry over medium-high heat for approximately 6 minutes. Add salt and sugar to taste to balance the flavors.

Serve the nasi goreng in a deep dish. Arrange the cucumber with the tomato along the side. Lay the fried egg (tjeplok) on top. Sprinkle fried onions over it.

TIP: Omit meat and shrimp paste for a vegetarian version.

8 ounces beef OR 7 ounces canned corned beef OR leftover meat from a previous meal
2 medium onions, chopped
4 cloves of garlic, crushed OR 1 teaspoons garlic powder
2 tablespoons oil OR 1 tablespoon butter
1 tablespoon leek, chopped
½ tablespoon celery leaves, chopped
2 teaspoon fresh terasi (shrimp paste), diluted with 4 tablespoons hot water
1 vegetable stock cube
1 tablespoon sambal oelek
½ tablespoon ketjap manis
2 cups cooked rice
salt to taste (start with a pinch)
½ teaspoon sugar
Garnish:
1 tablespoon bawang goreng (fried onions)
1 cucumber (run a fork along the length to score the peel, then slice thinly)
fried egg
1 tomato, sliced
krupuk (optional)

BOEBOER AJAM

RICE PORRIDGE WITH CHICKEN

This rice porridge was dished up to me when I was a child. It is also given to those who are ailing, as it is easily digested. Suitable for lunch as well as breakfast.

Clean the chicken and cut into pieces. Cook the rice in 5 cups of water together with the chicken. Add to this the celery, leek, stock cube and salt. When done, add the coconut cream. The rice should be slightly mushy.

Tip: Serve the boeboer ajam warm with a drizzle of ketjap asin and fried onions scattered over it. Serundeng also makes a good accompaniment.

*Chakway, or *cakwe*, are deep-fried Chinese bread sticks, also called *you tiao* or Chinese crullers, and may be available at Asian food markets or restaurants.

½ chicken
2 cups uncooked rice
½ tablespoon celery, minced
1 tablespoon leek, sliced
½ chicken stock cube
½ teaspoon salt
½ cup coconut cream
1 teaspoon ketjap asin
bawang goreng (fried onions)

BAMI GORENG

STIR-FRIED NOODLES

Cook the bami al dente and drain into a colander. Add 1 tablespoon oil to prevent sticking.

Sauté the onion and garlic in the butter until they are translucent. Add the pork and ham, and stir for a few minutes. Add the bami and vegetables, except the cabbage, and continue stirring. Add the ketjap manis and salt to taste. Just before serving, toss through the shredded cabbage.

Whisk the eggs with a little salt and pepper, and make an omelet. Allow the omelet to cool, then roll it up and slice into strips. Garnish the bami with the omelet strips and bawang goreng (fried onions).

14 ounces bami (dried egg noodles)
1 tablespoon oil
2 medium onions, diced
5 cloves garlic, minced OR 1 teaspoon
  garlic powder
2 tablespoons butter
8 ounces pork, sliced thinly
2 ounces ham, sliced thinly
1 tablespoon celery, sliced thinly
1 small red bell pepper, sliced thinly OR
  3 large lomboks (large chili peppers,
  deseeded)
1 tablespoon ketjap manis
4 cabbage leaves, shredded
2 eggs
1 tablespoon bawang goreng (fried
  onions)
salt and pepper

BIHOEN GORENG

STIR-FRIED RICE VERMICELLI

The basis of this dish is bihun, Chinese rice vermicelli, also known as mihun.

Cut the pork or chicken breast into bite-sized pieces. Soak the bihun in boiled water, separate with a fork, then simmer over medium heat for just a few minutes (the bihun should not get too soft). Pour out over a colander and drain the water off.

Sauté the onion and garlic in the butter until they are translucent. Add the liquid stock, leek, snow peas, small shrimp and pork or chicken, then add the ketjap manis and stock cube, and salt and pepper to taste. Now add the bihun, and stir well to combine evenly. Allow the mixture to continue cooking for 2 more minutes. Meanwhile, make an omelet with the 2 eggs, and cut it into pieces and add to the pan.

TIP: Add 2 teaspoons curry ground and 1 tablespoon sambal oelek to this recipe, and you've got Bihun Singapore.

1 pound chicken breast OR 1 pound pork (parboiled in 2 cups water for the stock), diced
14 ounces bihun
6 cloves garlic, pressed OR 1 heaping teaspoon garlic powder
2 large onions, sliced
3 tablespoons butter
1 chicken stock cube
2 ounces snow peas
4 ounces small shrimp
1 tablespoon ketjap manis
1 tablespoon celery
2 tablespoons leek, sliced
salt and pepper
2 eggs (for omelet)

INDISCHE MACARONISCHOTEL

MAC 'N CHEESE INDO DUTCH STYLE

Preheat the oven to 400° Fahrenheit.

Boil the elbow macaroni per the package instructions, then drain and allow to cool. Add a tablespoon of butter to prevent sticking. Chop the cooked ham into small dice. Whisk the eggs and add the milk, then crumble the stock cube into the milk and add nutmeg, and salt and pepper to taste.

Cover the bottom of a greased baking dish (approximately 1 ½ quarts) with a layer of macaroni, then a layer of ham and cheese. Pour over some of the milk sauce. Add another layer of macaroni, ham, cheese and sauce, and repeat these steps until the baking dish is full, ending with a layer of macaroni. Sprinkle the top lightly with the breadcrumbs and dot with butter. Place the dish into the preheated oven, and bake for approximately 30-40 minutes.

Tip: This dish can be prepared the evening before, and warmed up the following day in the microwave. Add sambal and/or chili sauce, and atjar (pickles) to taste.

8 ounces elbow macaroni
2 ounces butter
6 ounces cooked shoulder ham
5 small eggs
6 ounces milk
nutmeg
1 stock cube
salt and pepper
8 ounces medium-sharp cheese, grated
1 cup breadcrumbs

UITSMIJTER

DUTCH HAM & CHEESE SANDWICH WITH FRIED EGG

The word uitsmijter *means 'bouncer' in Dutch (literally: out-thrower). The story goes that this dish was served to bar patrons late at night, just before they were "thrown out" at closing time. This open-faced sandwich is often eaten for breakfast or lunch. The kind of bread and cheese can be your choice. The meat is often ham and the eggs are sunny-side up, yolks slightly runny. But in the end, how you eat it is up to you.*

Place two slices of bread on a plate and spread with butter or mayonnaise. Add the slices of ham and cheese.

Crack the eggs onto a heated skillet with butter and keep intact – don't scramble the yolks and whites. Fry the eggs on one side until the whites set and the edges begin to crisp. Place one egg on each sandwich.

Sprinkle with freshly ground black pepper and sea salt. Serve with a side of pickles and some sambal oelek.

TIP: Lightly toast the bread, add the ham and cheese then place under the broiler on high, until the cheese is melted and bubbly. Replace ham with roast beef or bacon.

2 slices of bread
4 slices cooked ham
4 slices of cheese, Edam or Gouda
    preferred
2 eggs
butter
mayonnaise
ground black pepper
sea salt

STAMPPOT BOERENKOOL

MASHED POTATOES WITH KALE

The Dutch love to mash their food. This stamppot is traditionally eaten in Holland during the winter. It is said that boerenkool (kale) tastes better after the first frost night of the season – end of November or start of December. We serve rookworst (smoked sausage) with our boerenkool and make a "jus-kuiltje," basically a little pool with gravy created on the top of the mash mountain. On cold winter nights this boerenkool hits the spot!

Remove the leaves of the boerenkool from the stalk. Wash and chop leaves finely. Boil the boerenkool in a pan with salt and enough water to cover the boerenkool and cook until done. Put the potatoes in a pan and add enough water to cover the potatoes by 1". Add a pinch of salt and bring to a boil over high heat. Simmer on medium heat until potatoes are done – about 15 minutes.

Cook the sausage in a separate pan until done. Mash the potatoes and boerenkool. Add stock cube, pepper and salt.

Preheat oven to 400° Fahrenheit. Place bacon slices on baking sheet. Bake until dark brown and crispy. Drain on paper towel and cool. Chop strips into small pieces and mix through the boerenkool. Serve with smoked sausage and gravy.

TIP: you can also use this recipe with raw endive or sauerkraut instead of boerenkool. The best Dutch gravy is freshly made with the browned bits that remain in the pan after the meat is taken out. Add 1 cup of water or red wine to deglaze the pan. You can thicken with roux – equal parts of flour and butter.

1 ½ pounds boerenkool (kale)
2 pounds russet potatoes, peeled, quartered
1 stock cube, diluted with 2 tablespoons hot water
pepper
salt
smoked pork sausage
8 slices bacon
gravy

HUTSPOT

MASHED POTATOES WITH CARROTS

Dutch one-pot meal made with mashed potatoes, carrots and onions for which we use the name hutspot. Some say the word comes from the French word hochepot or the English word hotchpotch.

This classic dish is often eaten as a main meal throughout the fall and winter seasons. Hutspot is also a traditional meal served during 3 October Festival in Leiden, the Netherlands. The festival commemorates the anniversary of the 1573-1574 Siege of Leiden (Leidens ontzet), during the Eighty Years War, when the Spanish Army attempted to capture the city.

Bring 2 cups of salted water to a boil. Add the beef and simmer for about 2 hours.

Cook the carrots, onions and potatoes (russet or red) in salted water for about 30 minutes, until tender. Drain the potatoes and vegetables.

Remove the meat from the pan and keep warm.

Mash together the potatoes with the vegetables and add butter and pepper. It should be thick enough for a spoon to stand up in it. Add some milk if too thick.

Serve with the sliced meat.

TIP: Serve with gravy the Dutch way: make a *'kuiltje'* (a small indentation) on top of the *hutspot* with a tablespoon, and pour some gravy into it. Instead of beef, serve with smoked bacon or sausage.

1 pound lean boneless brisket
salt
4 onions, peeled and sliced
2 pounds potatoes, peeled and quartered
2 pounds large carrots, peeled and sliced
4 tablespoons milk
fat
½ cup butter
pepper

PASTEI TOETOEP

INDO DUTCH CASSEROLE

Here is another one of our favorite comfort foods. My father used to make this simple casserole with ground beef and vegetables under a blanket of mashed potatoes. Toetoep is Indonesian for closed. Inspired by the British dish Shepherd's Pie, which is traditionally made with ground mutton or lamb, the ground beef variation is usually called Cottage Pie.

Preheat the oven to 350° Fahrenheit.

Boil the potatoes, drain when cooked. Mash the potatoes until smooth, adding a pinch of salt, dash of nutmeg, 1 tablespoon of butter and 1 egg yolk.

Mix 1 whole egg into the ground beef. Melt 1 tablespoon butter and brown the ground beef with the onion. Add the milk, salt, pepper, nutmeg, carrots, peas, corn, celery, stock cube. Cook for 5 minutes. Add soaked suun (glass noodles).

Boil 2 eggs. Transfer the ground beef mixture to a buttered ovenproof dish. Cut the boiled eggs into wedges and arrange them over the meat. Spoon the mashed potatoes over the meat, and press into the sides so that the filling is well covered. Even out the top using a fork. Whisk one egg yolk with some butter and spread over the pie. Bake the dish in the pre-heated oven for about 30-45 minutes.

Tip: As a variation, replace the ground beef with 7 ounces cubed, cooked chicken breast.

1 pound potatoes, peeled
½ teaspoon nutmeg
3-4 tablespoons butter
5 eggs
7 ounces ground beef
1 onion, diced
1 ½ cups milk
2 medium carrots, diced
7 ounces frozen peas
3 ounces frozen corn kernels
1 celery stalk, minced
1 chicken stock cube
1 ounce soaked suun (glass noodles)
1 tablespoon flour salt and pepper

SOUPS & SAJOERS

KERRIE LAKSA

CURRY SOUP WITH SUUN

Bring 6 cups of water to a boil with the half chicken, salam, sereh, and laos. When the water bubbles, turn down the heat to medium. Meanwhile, heat the oil and add the terasi, onion, garlic and kemiri, and fry until the onion is translucent. Add this herb mixture to the soup pot and mix well. Add the suun to the chicken and water, along with the stock cube and cream of coconut, and add salt and sugar to taste. Continue simmering until the chicken is cooked through and the oil has risen to the top.

To serve: Remove the chicken from the pot and transfer to a platter. Separate the meat from the bones, remove the skin and cut the meat into bite-sized pieces; discard the bones and skin.

Blanch the taugé briefly (about 5 minutes), then drain well in a colander until dry. Pour a serving of broth and some suun onto a soup bowl. Garnish with potatoes, taugé, eggs, chicken and celery, and sprinkle some fried onions over the top.

½ chicken
3 salam leaves (Indonesian bay leaves)
1 stalk sereh (lemongrass) (use the bottom 2 inches)
1-2" section of laos (galanga)
½ package suun (Chinese glass noodles)
1 teaspoon fresh terasi, diluted with 2 tablespoons hot water
1 slice fresh ginger, peeled and crushed
1 teaspoon kunjit (ground turmeric)
2 djuruk purut leaves (kaffir lime leaves)
2 onions, chopped
4 cloves garlic, crushed OR 2 teaspoons garlic powder
4 kemiri nuts, crushed
2 tablespoons oil
1 teaspoon salt
1 teaspoon sugar
1 chicken stock cube
⅔ cup cream of coconut
10 ounces taugé (bean sprouts), trimmed (tails removed)
1 small bunch celery, chopped (3 celery stalks)
3 hard-cooked eggs, cut into wedges
3 potatoes, boiled and diced
3 ounces fried onions

ERWTENSOEP

SPLIT PEA SOUP

This is a traditional hearty Dutch soup, also called snert and is made with split peas, vegetables and pork. Usually enjoyed throughout the fall and winter months. It is best when the soup has thickened (like porridge) overnight. Some prefer it so thick that a spoon can stand up in it. As my oma used to say, "Even back in the (Dutch East) Indies, we used to eat split pea soup with rice and sambal."

Bring 2 quarts of water to a boil with the stock cube, and cook the ham until well done. Remove the ham steaks from the broth, cut into bite-sized pieces, and set aside. Cook the soaked split peas until soft and they start to fall apart, then pass them through a sieve. Melt the margarine and sauté the onion, garlic and leek, then transfer to the broth with the celeriac, the sieved peas and the ham. Add salt, pepper and nutmeg to taste. Simmer for approximately 30 minutes.

Serve with slices of smoked sausage (optional).

1 pound pork leg (ham hocks)
1 beef stock cube
2 cups split peas
2 large onions, chopped
2 cloves garlic, minced
9 ounces leek, chopped
1 tablespoon butter
2 ounces celeriac (celery root), chopped
½ teaspoon pepper
½ teaspoon nutmeg
salt to taste
optional: 1 smoked pork sausage, sliced

BRUINE BONENSOEP

BROWN BEAN SOUP

This soup can be served as a complete meal, with rice and sambal terasi or sambal tomaat. A nickname for this is "BB with R" (brown beans with rice). A popular Manado dish is called brenebon, derived from the Dutch word bruine bonen.

Bring 4 cups of water to a boil with the chuck steak, stock cube and a dash of salt. Melt the butter and sauté the onion and garlic until golden. Add the bacon and leek, and fry for another 2 minutes. Transfer this mixture to the pan with broth and meat, and simmer until the flavors are absorbed. Last, add the sieved beans and mix well to combine. Simmer for an additional 5 minutes to heat through.

7 ounces chuck steak
1 beef stock cube
Salt
2 tablespoons butter
1 medium onion, diced
2 large garlic cloves, minced OR 1 teaspoon garlic powder
1 large can kidney/pinto beans, drained and sieved
4 ounces bacon, chopped
1 tablespoon leek, sliced into rings
½ teaspoon nutmeg

SAJOER ASAM

SOUP WITH TAMARIND

Bring 4 cups of water to a boil with the chuck steak, laos and salam until the meat is halfway done. Add the raw/unroasted peanuts and corn, as well as the kimiri nuts, shallots, garlic, lomboks, diluted asam and diluted terasi. Continue simmering until the meat is tender. Add the vegetables, and continue cooking until the vegetables are done. Add salt to taste. The sajur asam should taste gentle, mildly salty-sour; add sugar to round out the flavors.

Tip: Serve with a seafood dish and sambal terasi.

7 ounces chuck steak
2-inch piece laos (galanga)
3 salam leaves (Indonesian bay leaves)
7 ounces jumbo raw peanuts
2 large corncobs, quartered/cut into
    fourths
3 kimiri nuts
3 shallots, finely minced
2 cloves garlic, crushed
3 red lomboks (red chili peppers),
    roughly chopped on the diagonal
1 small chunk asam (tamarind) diluted
    with 2 tablespoons hot water
1 teaspoon fresh terasi (fermented
    shrimp paste) diluted with 2
    tablespoons hot water
10 ounces green beans OR 10 ounces
    katjang pandjang (garter bean/
    Chinese long bean)
¼ white cabbage OR melinjo leaves,
    if available
1 teaspoon salt
½ teaspoon sugar

SOTO AJAM
CHICKEN SOUP

This soup can be served as a complete meal or as a side-dish.

Place the chicken into a pot with 6 cups of water over high heat. Add the salam, sereh, jahe, laos, djuruk purut and stock cube, and bring to a boil, then lower the heat to medium and simmer. Grind the kemiri nuts, garlic, terasi and salt into a paste, then add the onion at the end and crush, retaining some of the chunky texture. Transfer these ingredients to the pot with the broth, and add the ground kunkit and sugar; continue simmering until the chicken is tender. Stir briefly to blend the ingredients. The flavor of this dish is on the salty side; the sugar rounds out the flavor.

To serve: remove the chicken from the pot (without the broth), and transfer to a platter. Separate the meat from the bones and cut the meat into generous bite-sized pieces; discard the bones. Blanch the taugé briefly until it is al dente (about 5 minutes), then drain well in a colander until dry. Place the eggs, potatoes, celery and taugé into soup bowl or on a platter with the chicken.

Pour the broth over and garnish with the fried onions.

½ chicken
3 salam leaves (Indonesian bay leaves)
1 stalk sereh (lemongrass) (use the bottom 2 inches)
1 slice fresh jahe (ginger), approximately 1 - 1 ½ inch diameter
1 medium section laos (galanga), thumb-sized piece
2 djuruk purut leaves (kaffir lime leaves)
1 chicken stock cube
5 kemiri nuts
5 clove garlic, grated OR 2 teaspoons garlic powder
1 ½-inch cube terasi (fermented shrimp paste)
1 teaspoon salt
2 medium onions, chopped
½ teaspoon kunjit (ground turmeric)
½ teaspoon sugar
10 ounces taugé (bean sprouts), trimmed (tails removed)
3 hard-cooked eggs, sliced into wedges
3 tablespoons celery, finely chopped
3 tablespoons fried onions

SAJOER GOEDEK

CHICKEN WITH VEGETABLES AND JACKFRUIT

This is a specialty from Djokja, the town my dad was born in. It's a soupy dish with chicken, vegetables and jackfruit.

Heat a generous layer of oil in a skillet and fry the chicken drumsticks until they are light brown, then drain on paper towel. Fry the tofu in the oil and drain on paper towel.

Add 2 quarts of water in a Dutch oven or soup pot and bring to a boil with the salam and laos. Once the water boils, turn down the heat and simmer.

Heat 2 tablespoons oil and sauté the onion and garlic until translucent. Add the kemiri, kentjur, ketumbar, djinten, diluted terasi, diluted asam and sugar, and stir well.

Transfer this bumbu (spice paste) to the pan with water, then add the tofu, chicken, eggs, nangka, santan and salt, and simmer over medium heat for approximately 5 minutes.

Last, add the vegetables and simmer until done, stirring occasionally. Gudek should be soupy and should taste somewhat sweet; add more sugar to taste.

1 pound chicken drumsticks
oil for frying
1 block tofu, cut into large cubes
2 salam leaves (Indonesian bay leaf)
1 slice laos (galanga)
2 large onions, chopped
5 large garlic cloves, minced
4 kemiri nuts, crushed
1-inch chunk kentjur (aromatic ginger / kaempferia galanga) OR 1 teaspoon ground kentjur
2 teaspoons terasi (fermented shrimp paste) diluted with 4 tablespoons hot water
1 small chunk asam (tamarind) diluted with 2 tablespoons hot water
1 tablespoon ketumbar (ground coriander)
1 tablespoon sugar
½ teaspoon djinten (ground cumin)
5 hard-cooked eggs
1 small can nangka (young green jackfruit)
1 cup santan (coconut milk)
1 teaspoon salt
¼ head cabbage, chopped
1 pound green beans, cut into bite-sized pieces

SAJOER LODEH

VEGETABLES IN COCONUT SAUCE

Heat 1-2 tablespoons oil and fry the tofu cubes lightly. Drain on paper towels and set aside.

Bring 4 cups of water to a boil. Add the cabbage, green beans, carrots, rebung, salam, sereh and laos and simmer until halfway done.

In a separate pan, heat the oil and sauté the shallots and garlic until light golden. Add the kemiri and the diluted terasi. Transfer this mixture to the pan with the vegetables, then add the green lomboks, tofu, peteh beans and coconut milk.

Stir occasionally to prevent the soup from separating, and simmer over medium high heat until done. Add salt to taste and round out the flavor with the sugar and ketumbar. This vegetable dish should be soupy; add a cup of water to thin, if necessary.

½ block tofu, cubed
½ head white cabbage, chopped
9 ounces green beans, in bite-sized pieces
2 medium carrots, sliced
3 salam leaves (Indonesian bay leaves)
1 stalk sereh (lemongrass) (use the bottom 2 inches)
1 medium laos (galanga)
5 kemiri nuts, crushed
3 ½ ounces rebung (bamboo shoots, sliced)
1 cup coconut milk
4 shallots, minced
4 garlic cloves OR 1 heaping teaspoon garlic powder
3 tablespoons oil
2 green lomboks (large chili peppers)
½ package peteh beans (fresh or frozen available at an Asian super market)
1 teaspoon fresh terasi (fermented shrimp paste) diluted with 2 tablespoons hot water
1 teaspoon sugar
½ teaspoon ground ketumbar (ground coriander)
salt

BAMI KUA A LA JESSY

MOM'S NOODLE SOUP WITH PANGSIT GORENG

This noodle soup is a perfect, complete meal. My mom Jessy served it with pangsit goreng (fried wontons), see recipe on page 173.

Melt the butter and sauté the onion and garlic until light brown. Add the ground beef; when done, add most of the leek, the sesame oil, ½ stock cube and pepper. Add salt to taste.

Remove from heat and set aside.

Bring 4 cups of water to a boil with 1 stock cube. When the water boils, add the rest of the leek, turn off the heat and set aside. Add salt to taste.

Beat the eggs with a pinch of salt, pepper and a little garlic powder, and make an omelet. When cool enough to handle, roll up the omelet and slice into thin strips.

Add the bami (noodles) to a pot with boiling water. Separate the strands with a fork, and simmer over medium heat until done. Drain in a colander and rinse with cold water. Add 1 tablespoon of oil and mix through to prevent sticking.

To assemble: Lay 1 lettuce leaf at the bottom of a deep soup bowl, then lay some cooked bami in the center of the lettuce. Pour some chicken broth over the bami; the noodles should remain visible, not be immersed under the broth. Spoon some ground beef on top of the noodles.

Garnish with a few strips of omelet, fried onions and spring onion. Place 3 pangsit goreng along the edge just prior to serving, so they remain crispy.

Tip: If you prefer pork, boil 3 ½ ounces cubed pork in 4 cups of water with 2 tablespoons fish sauce, and simmer for 3 minutes until done. Use this pork broth instead of the chicken broth. Add the cubed pork to the soup bowl along with the ground beef.

2 medium onions, chopped
3 cloves garlic, crushed OR 1 teaspoon garlic powder
1 tablespoon butter
14 ounces ground beef
3 ½ ounces leek, sliced
1 tablespoon sesame oil
1 ½ chicken stock cubes
salt and pepper
2 eggs
garlic powder
1 package bami (dried egg noodles)
1 tablespoon oil

Garnish:
4 leaves butter lettuce
2 tablespoons fried onions
1 spring onion, sliced
12 pangsit goreng (deep-fried wontons filled with seasoned meat) see recipe on page 173

SOP BETAWI

JAVANESE SOUP

This is a soup my aunt Nessy would make. Served over rice and always ready for a second helping.

Make a stock from the beef or chicken by simmering it in 4 cups of water for a couple of hours.

Heat the oil or butter and lightly fry the garlic and potatoes, then transfer these to the broth with the rest of the vegetables until everything is tender. If you are using the whole chicken, remove it from the pot; separate the meat from the bones and chop the meat, then return it to the pan, and add the vegetables (discard the bones). Add salt, pepper and nutmeg to taste. Add Maggi seasoning (optional).

Serve the sop djawa with a sprinkling of fried onions on top.

1 pound lean beef, cubed OR 1 whole chicken
4 cloves garlic, crushed
2 tablespoons oil OR 1 tablespoon butter
3 potatoes, peeled and cubed
5 ounces white cabbage, chopped
5 ounces carrot, large half-moon slices
5 ounces leek, sliced
5 ounces celery, chopped
½ teaspoon pepper
pinch of salt
½ teaspoon nutmeg
2 teaspoons Maggi seasoning (optional)
fried onions

SALADS & VEGETABLES

GADO GADO

VEGETABLE SALAD WITH PEANUT DRESSING

This cooked vegetable salad is one of my family's favorites. This is how it was always served at the restaurant, and is still made this way at home. It is suitable as a main course, a vegetarian option for lunch or dinner, and can also be served as a side dish. In Eastern Java it is prepared a little sweeter than in Western Java.

Prepare the dressing: Heat the oil, and fry the shallots and garlic until translucent. Add the sambal and diluted terasi, and while stirring, add the peanut butter and lemon juice. Simmer over low heat, and continue stirring to prevent burning. Water can be added if the sauce gets too thick -- it should not be too thick nor too thin. Add sugar and salt to taste; the sauce should be a little on the sweet side.

Prepare the vegetables: Bring a pot of water to a boil and blanch the vegetables separately, 3 minutes each; do not overcook, they should remain bright and crisp. Remove from the pan with a spider (perforated ladle), drain in a colander, and set aside. Bring the water to a boil before adding each new vegetable. Blanch the taugé for 30 seconds in hot water.

Serving and garnish: Place the vegetables in the center of a serving platter. Arrange the wedges of hard-cooked egg, tofu, cucumber and potato over the vegetables. Lastly, pour the peanut sauce over the vegetables. Garnish with fried onions and a piece of crumbled krupuk.

TIP: Serve with white rice or lontong (glutinous rice). Chill the rice, then cut into 1 inch slices. Vegan? Omit the eggs, and replace the terasi with ½ cube mushroom or no-beef stock, and the krupuk udang with emping (plant-based krupuk made from melinjo nuts).

For the dressing:
4 shallots OR 1 medium onion
4 cloves of garlic OR 2 teaspoons garlic powder
2 tablespoons oil
1 ½ teaspoons sambal oelek
2 teaspoons fresh terasi (fermented shrimp paste) diluted with 4 tablespoons hot water
4 tablespoons crunchy peanut butter
1 tablespoon lemon juice
Salt
1 tablespoon sugar, or 1 ounce gula jawa (palm sugar)

Vegetables:
½ head cabbage, shredded
7 ounces green beans, cut into 1 inch pieces
7 ounces fresh spinach
7 ounces taugé (bean sprouts), trimmed (tails removed)

Garnish:
2 hard-cooked eggs, sliced into wedges
4 slices of tofu, fried and cubed
½ cucumber, unpeeled, sliced
1 large potato, unpeeled, boiled, sliced
4 tablespoons fried onions
1 package krupuk udang (ready-to-eat is most convenient)

INDISCHE HUZARENSALADE

HUSSARS SALAD INDO DUTCH STYLE

I have fond memories of this purple-colored salad, the way my dad Billy used to make it. This refreshing salad was often served on warm summer days, with a baguette on the side. We would enjoy coming back for more throughout the day.

Season the steak with salt, pepper and nutmeg (or use the leftover daging smoor meat) and brown in some butter, then simmer over low heat. Boil the potatoes in their skins, and boil or roast the beets (or use pre-cooked beets). Peel the carrots, dice, and boil until slightly al dente. Boil the eggs, then set them aside in cold water. Warm the carrots until cooked. Chop the onion, peel the apples and dice both. Cut pineapple into small pieces. Peel and dice the cooked potatoes, beets and pickles, and cut the cooled steak into cubes. Place all these ingredients into a large bowl.

For the dressing: In a small bowl, mix the mayonnaise with the mustard and salt, pepper and sugar to taste. Little by little, add vinegar and whisk together. Taste and adjust seasonings if necessary. Pour the dressing over the ingredients in the large bowl and fold through well.

Arrange the lettuce leaves on a serving platter, and place the hussars salad in the center. Cut the hard-cooked eggs into wedges, slice the cucumber. Place these around the outside of the hussars salad like a garland. Finish off with a sprig of parsley.

1 pound lean flank steak, cooked (or leftover daging smoor)
salt, pepper, nutmeg
butter
7 medium potatoes
1 pound beets
4 ounces carrot
6 eggs
1 jar green peas or 1 package (10 ounces) frozen
1 large onion
4 large crisp sweet-tart apples, e.g. Granny Smith or Jonagold
1 cup pre-cut fresh pineapple
2 cups pickles
4 heaping tablespoons mayonnaise
½ tablespoon mustard
salt, pepper, sugar
vinegar
lettuce leaves
1 cucumber
parsley

KANGKOENG TERASI

WATER SPINACH IN SPICY SHRIMP DRESSING

Wash the kangkung, remove the hard stems and roughly chop the leaves. Heat the oil and sauté the shallots or onion with the garlic until translucent. Add the lomboks and the diluted terasi, and lastly the kangkung. The dish is ready when the kangkung is slightly limp and wilted down.

1 ½ pounds kangkung (water spinach, available at Asian supermarkets)
3 shallots OR 1 large onion, minced
3 cloves garlic OR ½ teaspoon garlic powder
2 tablespoons oil
1 teaspoon terasi (fermented shrimp paste) diluted with 1 tablespoon hot water
2 red lomboks (large chili peppers), deseeded and minced

LALAP

CRUDITÉ

These raw vegetables can be served as a side dish to the main meal. Often enjoyed with rice, baked fish, dry meat or chicken dishes, and served with sambal.

Wash the vegetables, cut to size and serve raw with sambal and lime on the side.

¼ head of lettuce
¼ head of cabbage
1 bunch katjang pandjang (string beans or garter bean/Chinese long bean)
½ cucumber
1 tomato
1 bunch basil
1 lime
2 tablespoons sambal oelek

SAMBAL GORENG TOMAAT

STIR-FRIED SPICY TOMATOES

For this recipe, follow the directions for Sambal Goreng Oedang Peteh. Replace the peteh beans and shrimp with 5 tomatoes. Cut the tomatoes into 6 wedges each, and stir them in the sambal goreng, and cook until slightly softened.

TIP: Sambal goreng tomaat is delicious as an accompaniment to grilled chicken or baked fish.

ORAK AREK

STIR-FRIED VEGETABLES

Shred the cabbage, cut the bell pepper into strips and the leek into rings. Slice the shallots or onion thinly, and sauté with the garlic until translucent in the butter, then add the shrimp. Add the cabbage, leek and bell pepper, stock cube and add salt and pepper to taste. Add the eggs and fold through until thoroughly dry and evenly distributed.

8 ounces shrimp, peeled and deveined
½ red bell pepper
½ head napa cabbage OR white cabbage OR 10 ounces haricots verts
1 tablespoon leek
4 shallots OR 2 small onions
3 cloves garlic OR 1 teaspoon garlic powder
2 tablespoons butter
salt and pepper
3 - 4 eggs
½ chicken stock cube, or 1 teaspoon chicken stock ground

SAMBAL GORENG BOONTJES

SAUTÉED GREEN BEANS

Fry the tempeh and tofu in the oil until light brown then remove from the pan and set aside. Wash the green beans and cut into pieces of approximately 2 inches in length. Mince the lomboks, onions and garlic as small as possible, add them to the oil and sauté so they begin to brown slightly. Add the salam, laos, diluted terasi and sambal oelek to the mixture. Keep stirring and folding until it becomes fragrant. Add the green beans and return the tofu and tempeh back into the pan. Add salt and sugar to taste. Finally, add the santan and water and simmer until the sauce is smooth and creamy.

1 package tempeh (8 ounces), cubed
½ block (6 ounce) tofu, cubed
2 tablespoons oil
9 ounces green beans
2 lomboks (large chili peppers)
2 small onions
3 cloves garlic OR 1 teaspoon garlic powder
2 salam leaves (Indonesian bay leaves)
1 slice laos (galanga)
1 tablespoon dried baby shrimp
½ teaspoon salt
1 teaspoon sugar
¼ block ¼ cup (concentrated coconut milk)
1 cup water
1 teaspoon fresh terasi (fermented shrimp paste) diluted with 2 tablespoons hot water
1 tablespoon sambal oelek

OBLOH OBLOH

PIQUANT VEGETABLE STEW

This spicy vegetable dish was served at the restaurant alongside bebotok (stewed meatballs), the first items to be mentioned while describing to our patrons, "Watch out for the bebotok and the obloh obloh!"

Fry the tofu and tempeh in a generous amount of oil and drain. Place the salam and laos in a large pot with the cut vegetables, and add water up to ½ inch over the vegetables. Boil until half tender. Sauté the onion and garlic in the oil. Add to the pot with vegetables along with the diluted terasi, sambal oelek, pili-pili, sereh, santan, water, salt and sugar. Stir gently and simmer over low heat until the oil rises to the top.

1 block (12 ounces) tofu, cut into large cubes
½ package (4 ounces) tempeh
3 salam leaves (Indonesian bay leaves)
2 slices laos (galanga, 1 ½ - 2 inches thick), crushed
½ head white cabbage, chopped roughly
5 ounces green beans, snapped into pieces
3-4 ounces carrot (1 large), sliced into half-circles
2 medium-large onions, diced
6 cloves garlic OR 3 teaspoons garlic powder
2 teaspoons fresh terasi (fermented shrimp paste) diluted with 2 tablespoons hot water
5 tablespoons sambal oelek
1 tablespoon pili-pili (small, red, dried peppers)
1 stalk sereh (lemongrass), use bottom 2 inches
1 cup santan (concentrated coconut milk)
1 cup water
2 tablespoons oil
1 teaspoon salt
1 teaspoon sugar

ROEDJAK MANIS
SPICY FRUIT SALAD

A refreshing fruit salad doused in a sweet and spicy dressing made from melted palm sugar, red peppers and sometimes crushed roasted peanuts as well. The ingredients can vary depending on the seasonal availability of the fruit. Another variation is to use tropical fruit such as fresh mango, belimbing (also known as carambola, or starfruit) and bengkuang (jicama).

Peel all the fruit and wash the unpeeled cucumber. Section the grapefruit, and slice the rest.

For the dressing: Pour 1 cup water into a saucepan and add the sugar, gula jawa, terasi, sambal (or finely chopped chili peppers) and a pinch of salt. Simmer for approximately two minutes, then add the diluted asam. Arrange the fruit in a dish and pour the dressing over it.

2 apples
1 grapefruit
1 belimbing (carambola, starfruit)
2 small hothouse cucumbers
1 bengkuang (jicama)

Dressing:
1 tablespoon sugar
14 ounces gula jawa (palm sugar) or
    brown sugar
1 teaspoon fresh terasi (fermented
    shrimp paste) diluted with 2
    tablespoons hot water
1 tablespoon sambal oelek
1 small chunk asam (tamarind) diluted
    with 2 tablespoons hot water
salt

OERAP OERAP

COCONUT VEGETABLES

Indo Dutch cuisine includes many vegetable dishes which are very suitable for vegans. This dish is simple to make, and can be served warm or at room temperature.

Bring a pot of water to a boil and blanch the string beans, taugé and cabbage until 'al dente'. Halve the cucumber lengthwise, remove the seeds and slice thinly. Mince the garlic and shallots.

Crush the fresh kentjur and djuruk purut and mix them into the diluted asam, diluted terasi, sugar and a pinch of salt. Bring ⅓ cup water to a boil and add the dessicated (grated) coconut; simmer until the water has been absorbed. Mix the bumbu (spice paste) with the coconut. Add the blanched vegetables and fold over until everything is evenly distributed. Serve on a plate.

7 ounces string beans OR katjang pandjang (garter bean/Chinese long bean cut into bite-sized pieces)
7 ounces taugé (bean sprouts), trimmed (tails removed)
½ head cabbage, shredded
1 cucumber, peeled
2 cloves garlic
3 shallots
1- inch piece fresh kentjur (aromatic ginger / kaempferia galanga) OR ½ teaspoon ground kentjur
1 djuruk purut leaf (kaffir lime leaf), sliced into thin strips
1 small chunk asam (tamarind) diluted with 2 tablespoons hot water
1 teaspoon fresh terasi (fermented shrimp paste) diluted with 2 tablespoons hot water (omit for vegan or substitute ½ mushroom/ no-beef stock cube)
1 teaspoon sugar
Salt
7 ounces unsweetened, dessicated (grated) coconut
1 tablespoon sambal oelek

TOEMIS SAJOERAN

SAUTÉED VEGETABLES

Separate the leaves of the bok choy and chop the firm bulb-end pieces into 1 inch diagonal pieces. Roughly chop the leaves. Sauté the onion and garlic in the oil until translucent. Add the snow peas, leek, bell pepper and the firm and leafy parts of the bok choy, along with the half stock cube, pepper and ketjap. Finally, add the taugé and sauté for just a few minutes so it remains crisp.

TIP: This goes well as an accompaniment to a spicy dish.

1 bunch bok choy
1 large onion, slivered
4 cloves garlic, minced
2 tablespoons oil
4 ounces snow peas
1 tablespoon leek, chopped
1 red bell pepper, sliced on the diagonal
½ chicken stock cube
½ teaspoon pepper
1 teaspoon ketjap manis
2 ounces taugé (bean sprouts), trimmed
   (tails removed)

SEAFOOD

MANGUT IKAN

FISH IN COCONUT SAUCE

Make a bumbu (spice paste) by crushing the shallots or onion, garlic, laos and lombok, and sauté in the oil. Add the diluted terasi, diluted asam and coconut milk, and cook the fish in this sauce over low heat. Add the djuruk purut leaf.

TIP: To compensate for the fishy smell when deep frying the mackerel, add some kunjit (ground turmeric) root to the pan.

3 red shallots OR 1 large onion, diced
3 cloves garlic OR 1 teaspoon garlic
    powder
½ - 1" section of laos (galanga)
1 green lombok (large chili pepper),
    sliced diagonally
1 teaspoon terasi (fermented shrimp
    paste) diluted with 2 tablespoons
    hot water
1 small chunk asam (tamarind) diluted
    with 2 tablespoons hot water
½ teaspoon salt
1 cup coconut milk
2 sole (plaice), fried
2 mackerels, cleaned, rubbed with salt
    and garlic and deep fried
1 djuruk purut leaf (kaffir lime leaf)

OEDANG WOTJAP

FRIED PRAWNS

This is my dad's favorite dish, and at his request, was put on the menu of our restaurant. It is my mother's specialty, and was very popular at the restaurant.

Peel the shrimp, leaving the tails attached. Slice along the back, and remove the dark vein with the tip of a knife. Mix the flour, garlic, ketumbar and salt and gradually add water until you have a thin batter. Wrap a slice of ham around each shrimp, leaving the tails exposed. Roll the ham- wrapped shrimp in the batter, and drain on paper towels.

For the sauce:

Sauté the garlic in the butter. Add the tomato ketchup, ginger syrup, sugar and water. Stir until dissolved, then add the vinegar and water. Taste to adjust the flavor balance: it should have a contrasting, gentle sweet-and-sour flavor. Add some water if it seems a little too thick.

For the garnish:

Lay a lettuce leaf on a platter, and spoon some white or yellow atjar along one side. Arrange 3-4 shrimp in the center, and pour the sauce over the shrimp.

6 jumbo shrimp OR 10 medium shrimp
3 tablespoons all purpose flour
2 cloves garlic, crushed OR ½ teaspoon garlic powder
⅓ teaspoon ketumbar (ground coriander)
½ teaspoon salt
5 ounces thinly sliced ham
oil for deep frying

Sauce:
2 cloves garlic, crushed
1 tablespoon butter
2 tablespoons tomato ketchup
2 teaspoons ginger syrup
2 tablespoons sugar
½ cup water
2 tablespoons vinegar
1 teaspoon salt

Garnish:
Lettuce leaves
White or yellow atjar

IKAN BALI

BALINESE FISH

Preheat the oven to 350° Fahrenheit.

Cut the fish into thirds. Sauté the onion and garlic in the butter. Add the sambal oelek, chili peppers, diluted terasi, ketjap and vinegar, mix well and add sugar and salt to taste. Warm the ready-made fish in the pre-heated oven for 10 minutes, then pour the sauce over the fish to serve.

2 medium pieces battered deep-fried cod fish
5 red shallots, minced
3 cloves garlic, grated
2 tablespoons oil
½ tablespoon sambal oelek
4 red lomboks (large chili peppers), deseeded and minced
1 tablespoon ketjap manis
1 tablespoon vinegar
1 teaspoon sugar
1 teaspoon terasi (fermented shrimp paste) diluted with 2 tablespoons hot water
pinch of salt

PEPESAN IKAN

BAKED FISH

Preheat the oven to 350° Fahrenheit.

Clean the mackerel, and remove the head and tail. Marinate the fish in the vinegar, salt and garlic 5 minutes. Heat a generous layer of oil in a pan and deep-fry the fish until light brown, remove from pan and drain on paper towel.

Cut the jahe into thirds. Crush the kemiri nuts, shallots and garlic and sauté the mixture in the oil. Add the jahe and tomatoes. Lay the fish onto a banana leaf and cover with the herbed sauce, then wrap by folding the sides in and fastening the packet with toothpicks. Aluminum foil can be used instead of the banana leaf.

Steam the fish for 30 minutes in a bamboo steamer, then place the fish in the preheated oven or on the barbecue to brown.

2 pounds mackerel
4 tablespoons vinegar
1 teaspoon salt
4 cloves garlic, grated OR 1 teaspoon garlic powder
oil (for deep frying)
4 salam leaves (Indonesian bay leaves)
8 kemangi leaves OR basil leaves
4 ounces lombok rawit (fresh chili peppers)
8 red shallots, minced
1 teaspoon sereh ground (ground lemongrass)
4 kemiri nuts, crushed
2- inch piece kunjit (turmeric) root OR 1 teaspoon ground turmeric
2-inch piece fresh jahe (ginger)
3 tomatoes, chopped
salt and sugar
1 banana leaf (available fresh or frozen at international markets) OR aluminum foil

SAMBAL GORENG OEDANG PETEH

SPICY SHRIMP WITH PETEH BEANS

This dish can be served on its own with a side of rice, but can also be part of a selection of dishes, wherein the flavor of the "stink" beans are quite distinctive.

Crush the onion and garlic with the mortar and pestle, then sauté in the oil with the sambal. Add the shrimp and simmer 1 minute to warm through. Cut the lomboks (or bell pepper) into thin, diagonal strips, and add these to the pan, as well as the santan (coconut milk).

Stir until well combined, then add the peteh beans, salam, djuruk purut, laos, diluted terasi, diluted asam, salt and sugar. Add water little by little when the coconut milk has thickened somewhat, and stir well. Simmer the sambal (sauce) until the oil rises to the top.

1 large onion, diced
6 cloves garlic, grated OR 1 teaspoon garlic powder
2 tablespoons oil
2 tablespoons sambal oelek
7 ounces medium shrimp, cooked
2 large lomboks (chili peppers) OR 1 red bell pepper, deseeded
1 cup santan
3 ounces peteh beans (stink beans/ bitter beans) (if using dried, soak in water overnight; fresh or frozen available at an Asian supermarket)
2 salam leaves (Indonesian bay leaves)
2 djuruk purut leaves (kaffir lime leaves)
2 slices laos (galanga, ½ - 1 inches thick), crushed
1 teaspoon terasi (fermented shrimp paste) diluted with 2 teaspoons hot water
1 small chunk asam (tamarind) diluted with 2 tablespoons hot water
½ teaspoon salt
1 teaspoon sugar
1 cup water

PINDANG KETJAP IKAN

SWEET AND SOUR FISH

Cut the mackerel into thirds. Marinate the fish in the vinegar, salt and garlic powder for 5 minutes. Sauté the onion and garlic, then add the sambal oelek, kunjit, laos and sereh. Stir continuously so it doesn't burn.

Bring ½ cup water to a boil with the ketjap, sugar, diluted asam and a pinch of salt, then add this mixture to the herbs. Add an additional scant ¼ cup water if the pindang sauce is simmering well and starts to dry out somewhat.

Heat the oil in a skillet and fry the fish for 3-5 minutes until done, then add the fish to the sauce.

1 medium mackerel (or another type of boneless fish)
2 tablespoons vinegar
⅓ teaspoon salt
½ teaspoon garlic powder (for the marinade)
1 tablespoon oil
4 shallots OR 1 large onion, diced
2 cloves garlic, minced OR 1 teaspoon garlic powder
1 tablespoon sambal oelek
1 teaspoon kunjit (ground turmeric)
2-inch piece laos (galanga)
1 stalk sereh (lemongrass) (use the bottom 2 inches)
3 tablespoons ketjap manis
1 tablespoon sugar
1 small chunk asam (tamarind) diluted with 2 tablespoons hot water

OEDANG TAOTJO

SHRIMP IN TAOTJO SAUCE

Heat the oil and sauté the lomboks, onion and garlic for approximately 2 minutes. Add the ginger, taotjo, sugar, salt and coconut milk. Last, add the shrimp, and simmer over low heat until the coconut milk has thickened. The dish is ready when the shrimp are opaque.

4 large lomboks (large chili peppers), deseeded and minced

4 green lomboks (large chili peppers), deseeded and minced

1 medium onion, diced

2 cloves garlic, grated OR 1 tablespoon garlic powder

2 tablespoons oil

2 slices ginger root (½ inch long)

2 tablespoons taotjo (fermented soybean paste)

1 teaspoon sugar

pinch of salt to taste (the taotjo is already quite salty)

1 cup coconut milk

8 jumbo shrimp (frozen shrimp have often already been cleaned and deveined)

MEAT, POULTRY & EGGS

BABI PANGANG

ROASTED PORK

Preheat the broiler to 300° Fahrenheit.

Score the meat, then rub in the salt, pepper and garlic powder, and rub brandy into the fatty top side. Marinate the meat for about an hour in the refrigerator. Place a baking dish half-filled with water into the bottom of the oven, then lay the meat directly onto the rack above it. Roast in the preheated oven until done, about 45 minutes. The meat is ready when the rind begins to blister and looks brown and crispy.

Prepare the sauce: Heat the oil and sauté the garlic. Add the taotjo, ginger syrup and tomato ketchup and 2 cups of water, then add the ketjap, sugar, vinegar and salt. Stir well until all ingredients are blended and dissolved, and the flavor is mildly sweet-and-sour. If needed, add a little water to thin the sauce; it should not be too thick. Cut the meat into ¾" thick slices, and pour the sauce over it.

2 pounds pork belly with rind
2 teaspoons salt
2 teaspoons ground pepper
1 ½ teaspoon garlic powder
1 tablespoon brandy

Sauce:
1 heaping teaspoon crushed garlic
2 tablespoon oil
1 tablespoon taotjo (fermented soybean paste, Indonesian variety, not Chinese)
2 teaspoons ginger syrup
1 tablespoon tomato ketchup
1 tablespoon ketjap manis
2 tablespoons sugar
1 tablespoon vinegar
pinch of salt

BABI KETJAP

BRAISED PORK WITH SWEET SOY SAUCE

The oldest recipe of Babi Ketjap was found in the cookbook Kokkie Bitja of the year 1854. A dish created by influence of the ethnic Chinese-Indonesians (Tionghoa-Indonesia). This family favorite is an easy recipe with tender pieces of pork and a fragrant soy sauce, served with rice and fresh cucumber sticks.

Cut the pork into cubes. Heat the oil and butter and sauté the onion and garlic. Add the meat and fry until halfway done. Add the jahe, ketjap and ketumbar. The sauce should not be too thick: add water to thin it out. Stir well to combine and simmer over low heat. Add sugar and salt to taste; the sauce should be slightly sweet.

1 pound pork belly
1 large onion, thinly sliced
4 cloves garlic, crushed OR 2 teaspoons garlic powder
1 tablespoon oil
3-4 tablespoons butter
2-inch piece fresh jahe (ginger), sliced lengthwise
1 cup ketjap manis
1 teaspoon ketumbar (ground coriander)
1 cup water
1 teaspoon sugar
1 teaspoon salt

BEBOTOK

STEWED MEATBALLS

This was one of our restaurant's signature dishes. For many years, my mother Jessy's recipe for these spicy stewed meatballs was a closely-guarded secret; many a fan would return time and again. It was one of Oma's favorites, enjoyed with a side of sajur lodeh, white rice and sambal. There were even some patrons who would purchase only the bebotok to go, and put them in their own Hungarian soup. When I came home from school, I would head straight for the kitchen, grab a bowl, spoon some rice into it, ladle tomato soup over the rice, then a great big piece of bebotok, and krupuk to top it all off. The South African dish bobotie *is said to originate from the Indonesian bebotok. Bebotok has its roots in the colonies in Batavia, the former Dutch East Indies, and is a specialty of the Cape Malays, an ethnic community in South Africa.*

Mix the ground beef with the onion, garlic, sambal oelek, kunjit, ketumbar, djinten, eggs, salt, sugar, red pepper flakes and ground paprika. Knead the mixture until all the ingredients are combined with the ground beef. Make three large meatballs.

Prepare the sauce: Bring 4 cups water to a boil over high heat. Add the laos, sereh, salam, sambal oelek, ketumbar, djinten, terasi, stock cube and kunjit, using the same amounts for the spices as in the meatballs. When the water boils, add the santan. Mix well, then add the meatballs to the pan. Simmer over medium-high heat until the meatballs are done (about 30 minutes) and the flavor of the soup has intensified.

2 pounds ground beef
1 onion, diced
5 cloves garlic, grated OR 1 tablespoon garlic powder
8 tablespoons sambal oelek
1 tablespoon kunjit (ground turmeric)
1 ½ tablespoons ketumbar (ground coriander)
1 heaping teaspoon djinten (ground cumin)
2 eggs
1 teaspoon salt
1 tablespoon sugar
3 tablespoons red pepper flakes
1 tablespoon ground paprika

Sauce:
1 piece laos (galanga), crushed to release the juices
1 sereh stalk (lemongrass) (use the bottom 2 inches), crushed
2 salam leaves (Indonesian bay leaves)
2 tablespoons sambal oelek
1 ½ tablespoons ketumbar (ground coriander)
1 teaspoon djinten (ground cumin)
1 teaspoon terasi, diluted with 2 tablespoons hot water
1 teaspoon kunjit (ground turmeric)
1 chicken stock cube
1 cup santan (coconut milk)

DAGING ROEDJAK

STEWED BEEF

Bring 6 cups of water to a boil and add the meat, along with the salam, laos and jahe. While this simmers, heat the oil in a wok and sauté the onion and garlic, then add the ketumbar, djinten, sambal, kemiri nuts, sereh, paprika, asam and terasi. Stir well while sautéing, then transfer this mixture to the pan with the meat and broth. Add the santan and another ¾ cup of water. Add the salt and sugar to round out the flavor.

Simmer until the meat is done and the oil rises to the top. The daging rodjak should not be too dry; add a cup of water if necessary. The meat should be submerged in the sauce. Omit the sambal oelek if you prefer the dish less spicy.

1 pound lean chuck beef, cubed (1 ½" x 1 ½")
1 piece laos (galanga)
1 piece jahe (ginger root)
3 salam leaves (Indonesian bay leaves)
2 tablespoons oil
2 onions, diced
4 cloves garlic, grated OR 1 heaping teaspoon garlic powder
1 tablespoon ketumbar (ground coriander)
1 teaspoon djinten
2 teaspoons sambal oelek
4 kemiri nuts, crushed
1 sereh stalk (lemongrass) (use the bottom 2 inches)
1 ½ teaspoon ground paprika
1 small chunk asam (tamarind) diluted with 2 tablespoons hot water
1 teaspoon terasi, diluted with 2 tablespoons hot water
1 cup santan (coconut milk)
1 teaspoon salt
1 ½ teaspoons sugar

DAGING SMOOR

BRAISED BEEF

Smoren is the Dutch word for braising, a cooking technique introduced by the Dutch way back when.

Bring 6 cups water to a boil with the half chicken stock cube, and simmer the meat until it is cooked and tender. Remove the meat from the pan; reserve the broth. Heat the butter and sauté the onion and garlic, then add the nutmeg, pepper and ketjap. Simmer over low heat. Add the cooked meat with 3 tablespoons of the broth and the vinegar. Add salt to taste. Stir until combined and add sugar to taste.

1 ½ pounds beef (skirt steak/flank steak), cut into 2 x 2 inch chunks
½ chicken stock cube
2 medium onions, sliced into ½ inch sections
4 cloves garlic, grated OR 2 heaping teaspoons garlic powder
3 tablespoons butter
1 teaspoon nutmeg
½ teaspoon pepper
4 tablespoons ketjap
½ teaspoon vinegar
pinch of salt
1 teaspoon sugar

DENDENG BLADO

DRY-COOKED SPICY BEEF

Heat the oil and pan-fry the meat briefly. Remove from the pan and drain on paper towel. When the meat is cool enough to handle, flatten it with a mallet. Sauté the shallots and garlic in the oil until translucent. Add the kebumbar, djinten, diluted asam, diluted terasi, laos, sambal oelek and sugar. Return the meat to the pan and stir well, then add the santan.

Simmer over low heat. The dish is ready when the oil rises to the top. The meat should be tender, the sauce rich and hearty. Add salt to taste.

1 pound 10 ounces beef, sliced into ½ inch x 2 ½ inch strips
2 tablespoons oil
2 shallots, minced
4 cloves garlic, minced OR 2 heaping teaspoons garlic powder
2 teaspoons ketumbar (ground coriander)
½ teaspoon djinten (ground cumin)
1 small chunk asam (tamarind) diluted with 2 tablespoons hot water
1 teaspoon fresh terasi (fermented shrimp paste) diluted with 2 tablespoons hot water
2 thin slices laos (galanga)
2 tablespoons sambal oelek
1 tablespoon sugar
½ cup santan (coconut milk)
½ teaspoon salt

EMPAL

SPICY SEASONED BEEF

Cut the meat into slices ¾ inch thick. Simmer the meat in a small amount of water with the salam, laos, diluted asam, ketumbar, salt and sugar. Keep stirring over low heat until the liquid has evaporated. Remove from heat and allow to cool. Flatten the meat using the pestle from the mortar and pestle until it is thinner. Fry the steaks briefly in hot oil.

1 pound beef (rump roast)
2 salam leaves (Indonesian bay leaves)
2 thin slices laos (galanga)
1 small chunk asam (tamarind) diluted with 2 tablespoons hot water
1 teaspoon ketumbar (ground coriander)
1 teaspoon salt
1 teaspoon sugar
½ cup oil

SATÉ KAMBING

MUTTON OR LAMB SATAY

This delicious satay has its own distinctive flavor and aroma. Drizzle the special ketjap sauce over the satay and sprinkle with bawang goreng (fried onions).

Cube the meat into ¾ inch squares. Combine the ketjap, garlic, salt and ketumbar to make the marinade. Coat the meat with the sauce and place in the refrigerator for 2 hours to marinate. Thread 3 cubes of meat onto each skewer and roast the satay over an open-flame charcoal grill for approximately 5 minutes, or 5-7 minutes under the preheated broiler.

Prepare the sauce: Melt the butter and sauté the onion and garlic over medium heat. Add the ketjap and lemon slices. Stir until the sauce has slightly thickened, then add 3 tablespoons of water. Do not heat for too long, or the sauce will taste bitter. Add salt, sugar and lemon to taste.

1 pound mutton or lamb
bamboo skewers

Marinade:
3 cloves garlic OR 1 ½ teaspoons garlic
   powder
1 tablespoon oil
1 tablespoon ketjap manis
½ tablespoon salt
½ tablespoon ketumbar (ground
   coriander)

Sauce:
1 onion, chopped
3 cloves garlic, minced OR 1 ½
   teaspoons garlic powder
1 tablespoon butter
3 ½ tablespoons ketjap manis
½ lemon, ¾ inch slices
½ teaspoon salt
½ teaspoon sugar

FRIKADEL PAN

INDO DUTCH MEATLOAF

This well-known meatloaf is in the top 3 of my all-time favorite dishes; my mother's version is irresistible and I would not ever turn down another serving. It is the ultimate comfort food: the fragrance and flavor brings me right back to my youth. This goes well with rice or potatoes, or the next day, between two slices of bread.

Preheat the oven to 350° Fahrenheit.

Place the ground beef in a bowl together with the onion, garlic, nutmeg, ground cloves, egg, salt and pepper. Knead the soaked bread into this until all the ingredients are combined. Place the seasoned ground beef into a buttered ovenproof loaf pan. Dot a little more butter over the top.

Place the pan in the middle of the preheated oven for approximately 30 minutes, then check to see if the crust has turned dark brown. Dissolve the half chicken stock cube in ⅓ cup of water and pour this with the ketjap over the meat just before turning off the oven.

1 ½ pounds blend of 50% ground beef and 50% other ground meat such as pork, lamb, turkey
1 onion, diced
4 cloves garlic, minced OR 2 rounded teaspoons garlic powder
1 teaspoon nutmeg
½ teaspoon ground cloves
1 egg
1 teaspoon pepper
2 teaspoons salt
1 slice white bread, soaked in milk
2 tablespoons butter
½ chicken stock cube
3 tablespoons ketjap manis

RAWON

BLACK BEEF STEW

Rawon is originally from Surabaya, a province of East Java. Rawon is usually served with rice, hence the name nasi rawon, served with raw taugé (bean sprouts), telor asin (pickled duck eggs), krupuk udang and sambal terasi. Its dark color comes from the keluak (black) nut. The fresh fruit and seeds contain hydrogen cyanide and are deadly poisonous if consumed without prior preparation. Be sure to purchase the pre-processed variety, as available at selected Asian grocery stores.

Make a broth by bringing 4 cups of water to a boil and simmer the meat, sereh and laos for approximately 30 minutes. With a mortar and pestle, crush the keluak nut with the shallots or onion and garlic. Sauté in the oil with the kunjit, ketumbar, terasi and salt, then transfer to the pot with the broth. Simmer over low heat.

To serve: ladle rawon into a bowl with some of the sauce. Arrange the egg, taugé, leek, celery and bawang goreng (fried onions) around the dish and serve with sambal terasi.

1 pound chuck steak or round-eye beef
1 stalk sereh (lemongrass), use bottom 2 inches
2 pieces laos (galanga), each approximately 1 ½ inches long
3 shallots OR 1 large onion, diced
4 cloves garlic OR 2 teaspoons garlic powder
1 teaspoon kunjit (ground turmeric)
2 keluak nuts, pre-soaked
2 tablespoons oil
2 teaspoons ketumbar (ground coriander)
1 teaspoon fresh terasi, diluted with 4 tablespoons hot water

Garnish:
2 hard-cooked eggs, sliced into wedges
7 ounces taugé (bean sprouts), trimmed (tails removed), blanched
1 tablespoon leek, minced
½ tablespoon celery, minced
bawang goreng (fried onions)

RENDANG

SPICY BEEF IN COCONUT MILK

A classic West-Sumatra (Padang) stew, which is also very well known outside Indonesia. Traditionally, rendang does not have a sauce. The process requires some patience, as the sauce should be entirely absorbed by the meat, giving it a dark color. When some of the thick coconut sauce remains, this dish is called kalio.

Cube the meat into ¾ inch chunks. With a mortar and pestle, crush the onion, sambal oelek, jahe, salam and kunjit. Place the meat and the spice mixture into a wok with 8 cups of water over high heat. Add the laos, sereh and djuruk purut to the wok with the santan. When the sauce simmers, turn down to low and continue cooking, stirring regularly to prevent burning. Remove from heat when all the liquid has been absorbed and allow to cool.

2 pounds chuck steak or round-eye beef
7 onions, chopped
2 ½ teaspoons garlic powder
5 tablespoons sambal oelek
1 piece jahe (ginger root, about 1 ½ inches long), sliced
5 salam leaves (Indonesian bay leaves)
1 rounded teaspoon kunjit (ground turmeric)
1 piece laos (galanga)
1 stalk sereh (lemongrass), use bottom 2 inches
4 djuruk purut leaves (kaffir lime leaves)
2 cups (coconut milk)

SATÉ BABI

PORK SATAY

Prepare the marinade: Cut the pork into cubes. Make the marinade by mixing the oil with the garlic, sugar, ketjap, ketumbar and salt. Coat the meat with the marinade and place in the refrigerator for 2 hours. Thread 3 cubes of meat onto each skewer and roast the satay over an open-flame charcoal grill for approximately 5 minutes, or 5-7 minutes under the preheated broiler.

Prepare the sauce: Heat the oil and sauté the onion and garlic. Add to this the diluted terasi, sugar, salt, peanut butter and 3 tablespoons of water. Mix well to blend. Add the ketjap and lemon juice. The satay sauce should be thick and quite sweet.

To serve: place 4-5 satay skewers onto a plate. Pour 1-2 teaspoons of peanut sauce over the satay, and drizzle a little ketjap over the top. Finally, sprinkle some bawang goreng (fried onions) to garnish.

Tip: to prevent the bamboo skewers from burning, soak them in cold water for 1-2 hours before use.

1 ½ pounds pork tenderloin or pork
   with a little fat
bamboo satay skewers

Marinade:
1 tablespoon oil
2 cloves garlic, crushed OR 1 teaspoon
   garlic powder
1 teaspoon brown sugar
½ tablespoon ketjap manis
½ teaspoon ketumbar (ground
   coriander)
1 teaspoon salt

Sauce:
1 onion, diced
2 cloves garlic, crushed OR ½ teaspoon
   garlic powder
1 tablespoon oil
1 teaspoon fresh terasi, diluted with 2
   tablespoons hot water
½ tablespoon sugar
1 teaspoon salt
4 tablespoons peanut butter
1 tablespoon ketjap
1 tablespoon lemon juice

Garnish:
bawang goreng (fried onions)

AJAM ANANAS

PINEAPPLE CHICKEN

Cut the chicken in half and score the legs. Heat a generous layer of oil in a skillet, and fry the chicken until golden brown and crispy.

In another pan, melt the butter and sauté the garlic, adding the pineapple and Maggi seasoning to brown, then add the pineapple juice. Remove the pineapple and set aside, and adjust the sweetness of the sauce with sugar to taste. Transfer the chicken to the pan with sauce to continue cooking. Pierce the chicken with a fork and spoon the sauce over the chicken periodically, so the sauce is absorbed.

Serve the chicken on a platter with the pineapple slices arranged over the top.

1 whole chicken
oil for frying
1 clove garlic OR ½ teaspoon garlic powder
2 tablespoons margarine or butter
4 slices pineapple, canned + 2 tablespoons of the juice
1 tablespoon Maggi seasoning
½ teaspoon sugar

AJAM SMOOR

BRAISED CHICKEN IN KETJAP

Heat the oil and fry the chicken pieces until done. Drain and set aside. Melt the butter and sauté the onion and garlic until translucent. Add the nutmeg, the chicken stock cube with ½ cup of water, the pepper and ketjap, then lower the heat. Return the chicken to the pan, adding the vinegar and cornstarch slurry. Mix until the sauce is blended, and add salt and sugar to taste.

1 whole chicken, cut into 6 sections
2 tablespoons oil
1 large onion, in ½ inch slices
4 cloves garlic, grated OR 2 heaped
    teaspoons garlic powder
3 tablespoons butter
1 teaspoon nutmeg
½ chicken stock cube
½ cup water
½ teaspoon pepper
4 tablespoons ketjap manis
½ teaspoon vinegar
pinch of salt
1 teaspoon sugar
1 teaspoon cornstarch, dissolved in 2
    teaspoons water

AJAM GORENG

FRIED CHICKEN

Dry-fried chicken marinated in garlic, vinegar and salt.

Cut the chicken into 6 sections, and score the flesh. Combine the vinegar, salt and garlic powder to make a marinade, add the chicken and turn to coat. Marinate for 1 hour. Fry the marinated chicken pieces in hot oil, and drain on paper towels.

1 whole chicken
2 tablespoons vinegar
1 teaspoon salt
1 teaspoon garlic powder
oil for frying

AJAM KALIO

COCONUT CHICKEN STEW

This dish has a rich, spicy and succulent sauce and comes from the Island of Sumatra and is inspired by Indian curry. Kalio is basically a rendang that is cooked half way, meaning there will be some sauce left (kalio is in the middle of gulai, like gulash, meat is done with more reddish, and yellow coconut sauce and in rendang the color should be jet black, very dry, the meat is hard and somewhat shredded and there is no sauce left). In restaurants kalio is often found and served as rendang.

In a wok (flat-bottomed wok), stir fry the onion and garlic until translucent. If using garlic powder, add after frying the onion. Add the kemiri nuts, kunjit, sambal oelek and stock cube and stir-fry over medium heat. Add the cooked chicken, with 1 cup of water, the laos, djuruk purut and santan. Continue cooking over medium heat, stirring occasionally. When the oil has risen to the surface, the dish is ready. Make sure some sauce remains; add more water if it begins evaporate too much.

2 onions, minced
3 cloves garlic, minced OR 1 ½
    teaspoons garlic powder
3 tablespoons oil
6 kemiri nuts, crushed
1 teaspoon kunjit (ground turmeric)
2 tablespoons sambal oelek
1 chicken stock cube
1 rotisserie chicken (store-bought
    roasted chicken), skin removed
    and cut into 6 sections OR 6 whole
    chicken legs (drumsticks and
    thighs), fried
1 small piece laos (galanga)
3 djuruk purut leaves (kaffir lime leaves)
1 cup (coconut milk)

I remember one time, a day before Christmas, when my mother had prepared a stuffed chicken at the restaurant, and had placed it into the large rice cooker to steam just before closing time. A short time later, her mother (my other Oma) came into the kitchen to get some rice for a last guest. I was in the kitchen as well, unsuspecting, occupied with another task, when my mother's loud scream caught my attention. In a fraction of a second I saw Oma Dee, who was not very tall, standing on her tip-toes, scrambling with her hand in the rice cooker. She looked surprised, because she could not see into the rice cooker but could not find any rice to scoop out, and kept bumping into something hard with the rice paddle. My mother had a look of shock on her face, and feared her ajam kodok had been battered: "Oh my ajam kodok, oh my ajam kodok!" she cried. I burst out laughing. Luckily, the ajam suffered no damage.

AJAM KODOK
STUFFED CHICKEN

In Indonesian, kodok *means "frog", alluding to the chicken's appearance when it has been deboned and cleaned. It is our family tradition to eat this stuffed chicken at Christmas Time, and is based on the British turkey recipe. The stuffing of poultry has its origins dating back to Roman times.*

Preheat the oven to medium/325° Fahrenheit.

With a sharp paring knife or razor blade, carefully debone the chicken, loosening the skin and separating the flesh from the cage; avoid making tears or holes. Keep the wings and legs intact and attached. Reserve the remaining scraps for another dish or make chicken stock from it.

Prepare the filling: Place the ground beef in a bowl together with the vegetables, garlic powder, shallots, cloves, cinnamon, nutmeg, ham, bread, raw egg, liver paté (optional), salt and sugar, and mix well to combine. Fill the chicken with the stuffing. Place the boiled egg in the center of the stuffing, so that when the chicken is carved, there is a piece of egg in each slice. Sew the end of the chicken closed at the tail end, and rub it all over with a little salt and pepper.

Lay the chicken into a buttered roasting pan and rub butter all over the skin, then place in the preheated oven. Baste the chicken regularly with its juices mixed with the ketjap, butter, salt and pepper, until a lovely brown crust appears. Pierce the skin periodically with a skewer, allowing the juices to run out to prevent bursting and to check doneness.

Tip: serve with roast potatoes, vegetables and compote/stewed fruit, or alternatively, with rice and sambal goreng boontjes.

1 large roasting chicken

Stuffing:
1 pound blend of 50% ground beef
    and 50% other ground meat
    such as pork, lamb, turkey
3 ½ ounces mushrooms, chopped
3 ½ ounces pickles, chopped
1 small can peas
2 teaspoons garlic powder
3 shallots, minced
½ teaspoon ground cloves or 4
    whole cloves
½ teaspoon ground cinnamon
½ teaspoon ground nutmeg
3 ½ ounces ham, chopped
1 slice white bread, soaked in milk
2 tablespoons butter
1 raw egg
salt and pepper
1 small can liver paté (omit if not
    available)
1 rounded tablespoon salt
1 tablespoon sugar
1 hard boiled egg

Marinade:
1 tablespoon ketjap manis
2 tablespoons melted butter
salt and pepper

AJAM TJOTJO

ROASTED CHICKEN LUCY STYLE

This savory and spicy chicken dish is originally from East Java and related to ajam bakar. This chicken dish is known for being slightly crushed or pierced with a fork (dicoco – new spelling). The chicken is best eaten with steamed rice and raw vegetables. Lucy Pustelnik has shared her family's favorite dish, which is very easy to make with local ingredients.

Cut the chicken in pieces and puncture with a fork. Marinate with salt and lemon juice and refrigerate for 15 minutes.

Preheat the oven and set the oven rack about 6 inches from the heat source.

Bake the chicken under the broiler for 30 minutes at 400° Fahrenheit until done (use a grill rack and pan with a dash of water to catch the drippings).

Heat the oil in a wok over medium heat and stir in the tomato paste, sambal oelek, brown sugar, chicken stock cube and the chicken drippings or water. Bring to a simmer add the chicken and put back in the oven for an additional 15 minutes until browned.

1 whole chicken
1 ½ teaspoons Lawry's seasoned salt
1 lemon - juice
3 tablespoons vegetable oil
1 small can of tomato paste
1 teaspoon sambal oelek (more to taste)
1 teaspoon brown sugar
1 chicken stock cube
1 tablespoon drippings of the chicken or water

SATÉ AJAM

CHICKEN SATAY

An uninformed customer once complained to Oma about the fact that his satay was burned. "Why don't you come to the kitchen with me," said my granny. The man followed her and she showed him an actual barbecue grill, on which the satay ajam was being roasted over glowing hot charcoal.

Preheat the broiler to 350° Fahrenheit.

Remove the fat from the chicken breasts (set the fat aside) and cut the meat into ¾ to 1 inch cubes. Combine all the ingredients for the marinade, add the chicken chunks and turn to coat evenly; marinate for 2 hours. Thread 3 or 4 pieces of chicken towards the center of the skewer, making sure that no wood is visible between the meat. Roast the satay over an open-flame charcoal grill for approximately 5 minutes, or 5-7 minutes under the preheated broiler.

Melt the reserved chicken fat in a small saucepan and mix this with the leftover marinade. Using a small brush, baste the satay with the marinade during roasting. The satay is ready when it is cooked through, and browned on all sides.

To prepare the sauce: Sauté the onion in the oil. Add the garlic powder, as well as the diluted terasi and the piece of terasi. Add the peanut butter, and 1 ¾ cup of water, as well as the ketjap, salt, sugar and lemon juice. Stir well to combine; if the sauce is too thick, add a little more water. The sauce should be a little on the sweeter side.

Tip: To prevent the bamboo skewers from burning, soak them in cold water for 1-2 hours before use.

1 pound chicken breasts
bamboo skewers

Marinade:
1 teaspoon garlic powder
1 tablespoon oil
1 tablespoon ketjap manis
½ teaspoon salt
½ teaspoon ketumbar (ground coriander)
dash of djinten (ground cumin), about ⅛ teaspoon

Sauce:
1 onion, minced
1 teaspoon garlic powder
1 tablespoon oil
1 teaspoon terasi, diluted with 2 tablespoons hot water
1 teaspoon terasi without water
2 tablespoons peanut butter
1 tablespoon ketjap manis
1 teaspoon salt
1 tablespoon sugar
1 tablespoon lemon juice

AJAM OPOR

SEASONED CHICKEN IN COCONUT MILK

Heat a generous layer of oil and fry the chicken pieces until halfway done, then remove from pan and drain. Fry the potato in the oil, drain and set aside. Place the chicken in a wok with 4 cups water and the salam, sereh, djuruk purut, laos and stock cube. Add the santan and simmer over low heat.

In a separate skillet, heat the oil and sauté the onion and garlic in the butter until they are translucent, then add the kemiri, ketumbar, djinten, terasi, asam, pepper, salt, nutmeg, sugar and cloves. Fold over several times to combine well, then transfer this herb mixture to the chicken in the wok.

Lastly, transfer the potato cubes and hard-cooked eggs to the chicken in the wok. Simmer a few more minutes over medium heat, stirring occasionally. When the oil has risen to the surface, the dish is ready.

6 whole chicken legs (drumsticks and thighs) OR 1 chicken, cut into 6 sections
5 medium potatoes, peeled and diced
1 sereh stalk (lemongrass) (use the bottom 2 inches)
3 djuruk purut leaves (kaffir lime leaves)
2-inch piece laos (galanga)
1 chicken stock cube
1 cup (coconut milk)
1 tablespoon oil
1 large onion, diced
2 cloves garlic OR 1 teaspoon garlic powder
6 kemiri nuts, crushed
1 tablespoon ketumbar (ground coriander)
1 teaspoon djinten (ground cumin)
2 teaspoons fresh terasi, diluted with 4 tablespoons hot water
1 small chunk asam (tamarind) diluted with 2 tablespoons hot water
1 teaspoon pepper
½ teaspoon salt
½ teaspoon nutmeg
1 tablespoon sugar
dash of ground cloves, about ⅛ teaspoon
5 hard-cooked eggs, peeled
oil for frying

BEBEK SUWAR SUWIR

BLACK-AND-SOUR CHICKEN

A traditional duck or chicken dish, often served in the Dutch East Indies as the main course for Christmas dinner. The name was simplified by Kokkie to sewarsewir.

Clean the duck or chicken and cut into sections. Season the pieces of duck or chicken with the pepper, salt and nutmeg and allow to rest. Melt the butter and brown the duck or chicken until golden, then remove from the pan.

Add the onion and sauté until translucent. Return the duck or chicken to the pan, and add the ground cloves, sugar, cinnamon, red wine, ketjap manis and a splash of water. Simmer the pieces of duck or chicken for about 2 hours, covered with a lid. Add the vinegar; the sauce should taste sweet-and-sour. Bind the sauce with the flour by combining 1 part flour and 2 parts water, mix well, then add.

Tip: This dish goes well with rice or boiled potatoes, with a side of red cabbage or stewed fruit.

2 young ducks or 1 chicken
1 teaspoon pepper
1 teaspoon salt
½ teaspoon nutmeg
4 tablespoons butter
4 medium onions, minced
½ teaspoon ground cloves
1 tablespoon sugar
1 teaspoon cinnamon
2 cups red wine
2 tablespoons ketjap manis
1 tablespoon vinegar
1 teaspoon all purpose flour

SAMBAL GORENG TELOR

HARD-COOKED EGGS IN SPICY SAUCE

This dish is easy and quick to prepare, and it is very tasty.

Crush the onion, garlic, terasi and sambal with a mortar and pestle then sauté this mixture in the oil. Add the salam, laos and santan, along with ¾ cup water. Add salt and sugar to taste. Cook for a few minutes while stirring, then pour over the eggs.

Tip: serve with white rice and a vegetable dish. Also an excellent accompaniment to rijsttafel.

1 onion, chopped
2 cloves garlic, sliced
1 teaspoon fresh terasi (fermented shrimp paste) diluted with 2 tablespoons hot water
1 teaspoon sambal oelek
2 tablespoons oil
2 salam leaves (Indonesian bay/ laurel leaves)
½ cup santan (coconut milk)
salt
sugar
3 hard-cooked eggs, peeled and halved

DADAR KEBERTOE

STUFFED OMELET

This Indo Dutch omelet is filled with seasoned ground beef. It is simple to prepare, and suitable for a main course or a side dish. Serve with a side of rice and a scoop of atjar (pickled vegetables).

Sauté the onion, garlic and kemiri nuts in the oil. Add the ketumbar, djinten, kunjit, diluted terasi, diluted asam and laos, then add the ground beef and mix well. Add the santan and flour when everything is cooked, then continue stirring and frying until the mixture is dry. Remove the laos (if using fresh slice).

Whisk the eggs with the garlic powder, salt and pepper and make an omelet. Lay the omelet on a plate, spoon the meat into the center and fold the omelet over the filling.

Tip: Drizzle some spicy chili sauce over the omelet, and garnish with fresh cucumber slices.

1 onion, minced
2 cloves garlic OR 1 teaspoon garlic powder
3 kemiri nuts, crushed
2 teaspoons ketumbar (ground coriander)
½ teaspoon djinten (ground cumin)
½ teaspoon kunjit (ground turmeric)
1 teaspoon terasi (fermented shrimp paste) diluted with 2 tablespoons hot water
1 small chunk asam (tamarind) diluted with 2 tablespoons hot water
1 slice laos (galanga), 1 inch diameter OR 1 teaspoon ground laos
2 tablespoons oil
½ pound ground beef
1 cup santan (coconut milk)
½ tablespoon all purpose flour

For the omelet:
3 eggs
½ teaspoon garlic powder
½ teaspoon salt
pepper

TOFU & TEMPEH

TEMPEH GORENG

FRIED TEMPEH

Set the sliced tempeh aside for half a day, or lay out in the sun until they look dry.

Mix 1 tablespoon water with the all purpose flour and rice flour to make a slurry. Gradually add the ketumbar, garlic, kentjur, ground turmeric, salt and egg. Mix to a medium-thick consistency, without any lumps.

Pour a generous amount of oil into a skillet, and heat over medium-high. Dredge the dried tempeh slices in the batter and fry to a golden brown.

1 package tempeh (8 ounces), cut into ½ inch slices
3 ½ tablespoons all purpose flour
5 tablespoons rice flour
1 ½ tablespoons ketumbar (ground coriander)
2 cloves garlic, crushed OR 1 teaspoon garlic powder
½ teaspoon ground kentjur (aromatic ginger / kaempferia galanga)
½ teaspoon kunjit (ground turmeric)
½ teaspoon salt
1 egg
oil for frying

BASO KOMBINASI

STEAMED SIOMAY

When my mother lived in the former Dutch East Indies, she would often hear the street vendor calling out, "Baso, baso!" He sold a selection of steamed tofu, cabbage, cucumber and potato, each filled with ground meat; my mother calls her recipe "baso combination platter." In Indonesia, this special treat is also known as siomay bandung, *derived from the Chinese word* shumai. *The Indo Dutch version is served with sambal katjang, a spicy, thin peanut sauce and lime.*

Crush the shallots, garlic and leek to a fine pulp and mix into the ground meat along with the egg, shrimp, salt, sugar and flour.

Slice the tofu into 2 inch pieces and then again diagonally. Fry these triangles in a generous amount of oil until golden brown, and drain on paper towels. Make a deep cut into the center of the slanted side, and fill the tofu with approximately 1 tablespoon ground meat, leaving some protruding. In the steamer, soften the cabbage leaves so they are pliable, then tell them with approximately 1 tablespoon of ground meat, and roll up. Hold the ends closed with toothpicks.

Boil the potatoes until they are just halfway done, cut in half, make a small hollow in the center and fill with a little ground meat.

Cut the washed but unpeeled cucumber into three equal parts. Slice in half lengthwise and scoop the seeds out with a spoon. Fill the hollow channel with a little ground meat.

Steam all the filled items in the steamer over medium high heat until the meat is cooked through.

To prepare the sauce: fry the kemiri nuts in the oil until light brown. Add the garlic powder, then the peanut butter and sambal oelek, as well as ¾ cup water. Stir until dissolved and well blended, then add the vinegar, sugar and salt. Add a little more water if the sauce is too thick. In general, the sauce tastes mildly sour, sweet and slightly salty.

2 shallots, finely chopped
3 cloves garlic, grated OR 1 ½ teaspoons garlic powder
1 tablespoon leek, finely chopped
1 pound ground beef OR a blend of 50% ground beef and 50% other ground meat such as pork, lamb, turkey
1 egg
4 ounces small, dried shrimp, crushed
2 teaspoons all purpose flour
1 teaspoon salt
½ teaspoon sugar
1 block (12 ounces) tofu
oil for frying
5 large cabbage leaves
3 medium potatoes
1 cucumber

Sauce (sambal katjang):
2 kemiri nuts, mashed
2 tablespoons oil
1 teaspoon garlic powder
1 ½ tablespoons peanut butter
2 tablespoons sambal oelek
4 tablespoons vinegar
4 tablespoons sugar
1 teaspoon salt

TAHOE TELOR PETIS

TOFU WITH EGGS IN SHRIMP SAUCE

A favorite dish of my uncle Koen's, and a very popular dish at the restaurant, especially among the non-meat eaters.

In a small saucepan, sauté the onion and garlic until translucent. Add to this the diluted petis, lemon juice, sambal oelek, ketjap, water and peanut butter and add sugar and salt to taste. Mix to make a sauce and keep stirring until all the ingredients are well blended. Add a little more water if the sauce seems too thick. The sauce can be on the sweet side.

Heat 1 tablespoon oil in a skillet and fry the tofu slices. Meanwhile, whisk the eggs with the leek, garlic powder, salt and pepper, then pour the egg mixture over the tofu in the skillet. Continue cooking over low heat and turn the omelet when the egg has set.

Bring a pot of water to a boil and blanch the taugé, drain well in a colander, then transfer onto a serving platter. Arrange the tofu omelet over the taugé and pour the sauce over it. Sprinkle the celery, fried onions and crumbled krupuk over the top.

3 shallots, finely chopped
3 cloves garlic, grated
2 tablespoons oil
1 teaspoon petis (shrimp paste), diluted with 2 tablespoons hot water (omit for vegan or substitute ½ mushroom/no-beef stock cube)
1 teaspoon lemon juice
1 ½ teaspoons sambal oelek
2 tablespoons ketjap manis
2 tablespoons water
2 tablespoons peanut butter
1 ½ teaspoons sugar
Salt
½ block (6 ounces) tofu, sliced into ½ inch slabs, then into 4 pieces
2 eggs
1 tablespoon leeks, finely chopped
½ teaspoon garlic powder
7 ounces taugé (bean sprouts), trimmed (tails removed)
1 tablespoon celery, finely chopped
1 tablespoon fried onions
1 handful krupuk

BALE PAMEREMAN

SNACKS & SIDE DISHES

PANGSIT GORENG

DEEP-FRIED WONTONS FILLED WITH MEAT MIXTURE

This was always a popular appetizer at the restaurant, and is still a big hit at parties. The light and crispy wonton wrappers have a flavorful filling, and also go well with Bami Kua.

Prepare the filling: In a bowl, combine the ground meat with the shrimp, leek, garlic powder, egg yolk, salt and pepper. Place 1 teaspoon of filling into the center of a wrapper. Fold one corner up and over the filling, almost to the top, and press gently to close. Turn the package over pointing down. Take the 2 outer corners and fold these up, then stick them together into a triangle with a dab of beaten egg, or a slurry of flour and water. Repeat with all the pastry sheets. Heat the oil, and fry the pangsit until golden brown, then drain on paper towels.

Prepare the *dipping* sauce: Melt the butter and sauté the garlic. Add the tomato ketchup, ginger syrup, sugar and ⅓ cup water; continue stirring until the sugar has dissolved. Add the vinegar and salt, then taste the sauce: it should have a mildly sour and sweet flavor. Add a little water if the consistency is too thick.

1 package square wonton wrappers (available at Asian grocery stores) OR cut larger spring roll wrappers (6-inch squares) into quarters. You will need 64 wrappers for 14 ounces of ground beef.
1 egg, beaten
oil for frying

Filling:
14 ounces ground beef OR a blend of 50% ground beef and 50% other ground meat such as pork, lamb, turkey
3 ½ ounces small shrimp, mashed
1 tablespoon leek, chopped and crushed
½ teaspoon garlic powder
1 egg yolk
1 teaspoon salt
½ teaspoon pepper

Dipping Sauce:
1 teaspoon garlic, crushed
1 tablespoon butter
1 tablespoon tomato ketchup
2 teaspoons ginger syrup
1 ½ tablespoons sugar
2 tablespoons vinegar
1 teaspoon salt

SAUCIJZENBROODJES

DUTCH SAUSAGE ROLLS

These tasty sausages wrapped in puff pastry can be enjoyed as a snack with some mustard or chili sauce for dipping. My wife Petra Davidson loves this for breakfast, lunch or dinner.

Preheat the oven to 450° Fahrenheit.

Season the ground beef with the hamburger seasoning, ground coriander, cinnamon, nutmeg, salt and pepper, milk and chicken liver pate and knead well to combine. Divide into 10 portions and roll into cylinders approximately 3 inches long, using breadcrumbs if desired. Brush a little water around the edges of a puff pastry square, then lay a sausage in the center and fold the dough around it, leaving the ends open. Repeat with all pastry squares. Lay the sausage rolls on a baking sheet lined with baking parchment, 1 inch apart. Brush the beaten egg yolk over the top, and bake in the center of a preheated oven for 35-40 minutes until done.

Filling variation: add 1 teaspoon curry ground and 1 crushed garlic clove.

Tip: Make croutons from sliced sausage rolls. Cut the sausage rolls into thirds, sprinkle with grated mature cheese, and bake in the oven for 20-25 minutes.

10 ounces ground beef
1 teaspoon hamburger seasoning
1 teaspoon ground coriander
½ teaspoon cinnamon
½ teaspoon nutmeg
salt and pepper
1 tablespoon milk
breadcrumbs (optional)
1 package frozen puff pastry, cut into
	squares of approximately 4" x 4"
1 egg, separated, yolk beaten
1 small can chicken liver pate
baking parchment

BAKPAO

STEAMED BUNS FILLED WITH GROUND PORK

These Chinese steamed buns with meat or chicken filling are delicious as a snack with a dollop of sambal or garlic-chili sauce. My uncle John and aunt Rora regularly took me to their favorite restaurant in New York's Chinatown which had the very best bakpao. We would buy an entire bag, and devour them in the car.

Prepare the filling: Heat the butter and sauté the onion and garlic. Add the leek, celery, ground pork, ketjap, sugar, and a dash of salt and pepper. Stir well over low heat until done. Remove from heat until cooled off, then cover and set aside in the refrigerator. The mixture should be firm and cold before using as filling.

For the dough: dissolve the yeast in the lukewarm milk. Add the flour a little at a time, followed by the butter, sugar and eggs, and add salt to taste. Knead the dough thoroughly, until it is smooth and supple. Roll the dough into a log approximately 2 ½ - 3 inches thick, then cut into 1 inch slices. Heap 2 teaspoons of filling into the center of each slice, and close the dough around the filling. Place each bun onto a sheet of wax paper, and allow to rise for 1 hour. Steam the bakpao with the paper (to avoid sticking) in a bamboo steamer for 10 minutes until done.

Filling:
1 onion, diced
5 cloves garlic, crushed
1 tablespoon butter
1 tablespoon leek, chopped
1 tablespoon celery, chopped
5 ounces ground pork
3-4 tablespoons ketjap manis
1 tablespoon sugar
salt and pepper

Dough:
1 package (¼ ounce) active dry yeast
1 ½ cups lukewarm milk
3 cups all purpose flour
1 tablespoon butter
1 tablespoon sugar
1-2 eggs
salt
wax/greaseproof paper, cut into 2 x 2 inch squares

INDO-DUTCH KROKET

POTATO CROQUETTES FILLED WITH GROUND BEEF

Boil the potatoes, remove the skin after cooking. Mash the potatoes until smooth and lump-free and add the salt. Sauté the shallots and garlic until translucent. Add the ground beef, 1 tablespoon beaten egg, carrots, leek, pepper and sugar, and add salt to taste. When the mixture is cooked, remove from heat and stir in the ketjap.

Place 1 tablespoon mashed potatoes onto a plate and flatten to 1 ½ inch thickness. Lay a half teaspoon of filling on top, then roll into a cylinder. Dip the croquette in the beaten egg, then roll in the breadcrumbs until coated. Heat a generous layer of oil in a skillet, and carefully fry the croquettes until golden brown.

1 ¾ pounds potatoes
½ teaspoon salt
4 shallots, minced
3 cloves garlic, minced
1 tablespoon butter
7 ounces ground beef
2 eggs, beaten
7 ounces carrots, diced
1 teaspoon ketjap manis
7 ounces breadcrumbs
1 tablespoon leek, minced
½ teaspoon pepper
pinch of sugar
oil for frying

FRIKADEL DJAGOENG

DEEP-FRIED CORN FRITTERS

Slice the corn kernels from the cobs, and scrape the cobs to remove any leftover kernels as well as the milky residue. Combine with the onion, garlic, salt, pepper, ketumbar, sugar, egg, leek or celery, flour and shrimp. If desired, add the sambal oelek. If you are using canned sweet corn, drain, then mash briefly. In a skillet, heat a generous layer of oil. Take a spoonful of the corn mixture and form into a flat patty. Slide the patty off the spoon with a knife and lower carefully into the hot oil. Fry the corn fritters until light golden brown.

4 fresh corncobs (not too young) OR 1 12-ounce can sweet corn (10 ounces drained)
1 shallot OR 1 small onion, minced
3 cloves garlic, crushed OR 1 teaspoon garlic powder
½ teaspoon salt
½ teaspoon pepper
1 teaspoon ketumbar (ground coriander)
½ teaspoon sugar
1 egg
1 tablespoon leek, minced OR 1 tablespoon celery, minced
4 tablespoons self-rising flour
3 ounces small shrimp, rough-mashed
1 ½ teaspoons sambal oelek (for spicy corn fritters)
oil for deep-frying

FRIKADEL KENTANG

FRIED POTATO PATTIES

These savory potato patties (also known as perkedel) are a perfect snack or suitable as a side dish to a main course. The name originates from frikadeller or frikadellen (not to be confused with the traditional Dutch frikadel); historically, it was a fried meat ball, but can also be flattened into a disc. It can be found in Denmark, Germany, Poland, Belgium and The Netherlands, in one form or another. The standard, traditional ingredients are ground pork or beef, minced onions, egg, milk, bread crumbs, salt and pepper; in the Indo Dutch version, it is a mixture of mashed potatoes and ground beef or canned corned beef.

Boil the potatoes, remove the skin after cooking. Mash the potatoes and combine with the ground beef, leek, celery, eggs, nutmeg, pepper and salt. Make flat, round discs: roll into small balls about the size of a ping pong ball, then flatten gently to 1 inch thickness. Loosen the egg yolks with a fork, then roll each disc into the egg yolk. Fry in hot oil until golden brown.

Tip: replace the ground beef with 4 ounces of small shrimp.

1 pound potatoes
4 ounces ground beef
1 tablespoon leek, chopped
1 tablespoon celery, chopped
2 eggs
1 teaspoon nutmeg
½ teaspoon pepper
1 teaspoon salt
2 egg yolks
oil for frying

PASTEITJES
INDO DUTCH FILLED PASTRY

This is a popular Indo Dutch snack, called pastel in Indonesia. Inspired by Cornish Pasties from England, pastel is deep-fried and has a thin, crispy crust, and is folded closed into a half-moon shape. Pastel is often filled with small cubes of chicken, potato, carrot, onion, peas, garlic and white pepper. Some recipes also include suun (glass noodles). Another variation is the panada, *which comes from empanada, originating in Galicia (northwest Spain) and Portugal. The word empanada is derived from the verb* empanar, *meaning wrapped or enveloped in dough. Tuna is commonly used as a filling for panada. Just like the pasteitje, the panada is baked in the oven, but is smaller, so it is easy to eat on the go. It is presumed that the empanada is related to the* calzone *(Italian) and* samosa *(Arabic/Indian).*

Prepare the filling: Melt the butter in a skillet and sauté the onion for about 30 seconds. Add the ground beef and continue cooking for about 5 minutes while stirring. Add the ketjap, nutmeg and sugar; add salt and pepper to taste. Add the water, lower the heat and simmer until the meat is somewhat dry. Sprinkle the flour over the ground beef and mix in. Boil the carrots briefly. Bring some water to a boil and cook for 3 minutes, then drain in a colander. Add the cooked carrots, suun and celery to the meat mixture.

For the crust: Combine the flour, salt, egg, margarine/butter and ½ cup water and knead into a supple dough. Roll the dough out, fold it over twice into a square and then cut it into 2. Roll the pieces out into narrow strips 1 inch thick. Cut out circles of approximately 3 inches in diameter. For each circle of dough, place a heaping tablespoon of filling in the center with a slice of egg. Wet the edge of the pastry circle with a brush and fold over to close. Press the edges together well, and fold over. Fry the pastries in oil until golden brown.

Filling:
½ tablespoon margarine OR butter
1 onion, chopped
9 ounces ground beef or ground turkey
2 tablespoons ketjap manis
½ teaspoon nutmeg
1 teaspoon sugar
2 tablespoons water
salt and pepper
½ tablespoon all purpose flour
3 tablespoons carrots, minced
3 tablespoons peas
1 ounce (small handful) suun (Chinese glass noodles)
1 tablespoon celery, chopped
2 hard-cooked eggs, sliced
oil for frying

Crust:
3 ⅓ cups all purpose flour
pinch of salt
1 egg
1 stick of butter

LOEMPIA

INDO DUTCH SPRING ROLLS

The best loempia is generously filled and has a thin and crispy crust. Special pliable wrappers can be found fresh or frozen at Asian supermarkets. Use the larger wrappers (8 x 8 inches square). In the Netherlands a large loempia is served as a light meal.

Using a mortar and pestle, crush the onion and garlic, and sauté in the oil. Add the pork, chicken breast, shrimp and ham, and stir for 2 minutes. Add the leek, celery, bamboo shoots and cabbage and continue cooking for 3 more minutes. Add the taugé, salt and pepper and mix well to combine. Remove from heat and allow to cool; the mixture should be completely cooled off before using. Lay one spring roll wrapper on a clean, dry surface with a corner towards you and spoon 2 tablespoons of filling along the center. Brush the outer edges of the wrapper with a dab of beaten egg yolk. Fold the bottom corner of the wrapper over the filling and press lightly. Take the right corner and fold towards the center. Repeat with the left side, so it looks like an envelope, then roll the lumpia over to close. Heat a generous layer of oil to approximately 350 degrees Fahrenheit and fry the lumpias to a golden brown, about 5 minutes. Make sure the lumpias are completely immersed in the oil, otherwise the wrapper could burst. Drain on paper towels. Serve with sambal or chili sauce.

Tip: Lay a smaller square, a quarter wrapper, in the center of the larger spring roll wrapper for reinforcement, to prevent the lumpia from bursting open during frying. Spoon the filling onto the smaller wrapper, and fold the smaller wrapper over the filling like an envelope. Then wrap the larger wrapper as described above. Drape a damp tea towel over the unused defrosted wrappers to prevent drying and keep them pliable.

1 onion
3 cloves garlic
oil
5 ounces pork, chopped small
3 ounces chicken breast, chopped small
3 ounces shrimp
3 slices ham, shredded
1 tablespoon leek, julienned
1 tablespoon celery
1 small can bamboo shoots, julienned
5 ounces taugé (bean sprouts), trimmed (tails removed)
salt and pepper to taste
3 ounces cabbage, shredded
4 spring roll wrappers
1 egg yolk, beaten
oil for deep frying

REMPEJEK KATJANG

PEANUT CRACKERS

This crunchy deep-fried vegetarian crisp with peanuts is something that my friend Michael Passage cannot get enough of. This savory snack, originally from Java, is often served as a side dish and also makes an excellent cocktail party snack. This recipe makes about 40 – 50. Store in airtight container.

Combine rice flour, egg, coconut milk, baking soda, ketumbar, kentjur, djinten, garlic, lime leaves and salt together and stir until evenly distributed and smooth.

The batter has to be watery – so add one tablespoon or more coconut milk or water when needed.

Heat the oil in a wok over medium heat.

Pour the mixture with a small ladle against the side of the wok, just above the level of the hot oil to form a thin disk. Make 2 or 3 around the wok. Let the rempeyek fry 1 minute and then scrape them off the side and let them float in the oil to fry for another minute or two and turn them over until golden brown. Remove and drain on paper towel.

2 cups rice flour
1 ½ cups coconut milk
1 egg, beaten
¼-½ teaspoon baking soda
1 teaspoon ground ketumbar
   (coriander)
½ teaspoon ground kentjur (aromatic
   ginger / kaempferia galangal)
½ teaspoon ground djinten (cumin)
2 cloves garlic
5 pieces of lime leaves, thinly sliced
pinch of salt
2 cups peanuts
2 cups oil for frying

LEMPER AJAM

CHICKEN-FILLED RICE ROLLS

A rice roll filled with seasoned shredded chicken, wrapped in plastic wrap.
This dish can be made more flavorful by wrapping in a piece of banana leaf,
and roasting over an open flame for a few minutes. Great snack for
any occasion.

Cook the chicken breast in water until done, then shred the meat with a
fork and chop into smaller pieces. Place the ketan (sticky) rice in a pan
of water, where the water is 1 inch above the surface of the rice, and boil
with 2 cups of santan. [In my grandmother's original recipe, the rice is first
soaked in water for several hours, then steamed and coconut milk added].

Heat 1-2 tablespoons oil and fry the onion and garlic over low heat until
crispy, then add the chicken, ketumbar, djinten, djuruk purut, kemiri,
sereh, kentjur, remaining 1 cup of santan and stock cube, and add salt and
pepper to taste, with a little sugar to round out the flavors. Mix well to
combine and simmer until the coconut milk has been absorbed.

To make the rolls: cut plastic wrap in 4 x 4 inch squares; each lemper will
be 2-3 inches long. Spoon some ketan rice over the plastic wrap, then fold
the plastic wrap over and flatten the rice to make it a little bigger, to a
width of 2-3 inches. Fold the plastic wrap back and place 1 tablespoon of
filling along the center. Grab the lower edge of the plastic wrap and fold
it over to the top edge, so the rice does not stick to your fingers. Pinch the
opening closed with your fingers. Wrap the plastic compactly around the
rice to shape into a cylinder. Roll the plastic wrap closed. Twist the sides
closed to make a snug roll. Fold the ends of the twisted plastic wrap neatly
in. Steam the rolls in a steamer for approximately 10 minutes. Serve warm
or at room temperature.

12 ounces chicken breast
2 cups ketan (sticky) rice, not to be
    confused with lontong rice
3 cups santan, divided
3 cloves garlic, minced
2 medium onions, minced oil
1 tablespoon kebumbar (ground
    coriander)
1 teaspoon djinten
2 djuruk purut leaves (kaffir lime
    leaves)
5 kemiri nuts, crushed
1 stalk sereh (lemongrass), use
    bottom 2 inches
½ teaspoon ground kentjur
    (aromatic ginger / kaempferia
    galangal)
1 cup water
1 chicken stock cube
salt and pepper to taste
1 tablespoon sugar
plastic wrap

RISOLLES

RAGOUT-FILLED CREPES

The name of this dish derives from the French word "risoller", a cooking technique where food is fried to give it a crispy golden crust. Risolles were introduced by the Portuguese and evolved into one of the most popular Indo Dutch snacks: a folded crepe filled with chicken, carrot, potato and beans, or a chicken/beef ragout filling, covered in breadcrumbs and deep-fried. They are traditionally served with a chili sauce. The recipe below is my mother Jessica's own, she uses chicken or beef ragout. They are irresistible!

Prepare the ragout: Melt the butter and sauté the onion until translucent. Crumble in the ground beef. Add the leek, celery, carrot and garlic powder and stir well. When the meat is browned and the mixture is combined evenly, pour in the milk, allowing the meat to float freely in the liquid.

Simmer for a few minutes, stirring constantly, then add the flour to thicken the sauce. Add the stock cubes, nutmeg and salt to taste, then add the sugar to round out the flavor; it should taste somewhat sweet. Stir the mixture well to combine, and set aside to cool completely.

Prepare the batter: Make a batter with the flour, milk, one egg and a pinch of salt. Use a 6 inch non-stick skillet to make the crepes. The crepes should be soft and limp enough to roll.

Place one tablespoon of filling near the lower edge of the crepe. Fold the bottom over towards the top. Then fold in the right and left sides and roll up to close. Seal the end with a dab of batter and press closed. Beat the second egg, and roll the crepe packet in the egg, then in the breadcrumbs to coat. Heat oil to around 355° Fahrenheit and fry the risolles until golden brown. Serve with mustard or chili sauce; sambal katjang also goes well (see baso kombinasi, 166).

Ragout:
2 onions, minced
2 teaspoons garlic powder
2 tablespoons butter
14 ounces ground beef
1 leek, chopped
4 celery stalks, chopped
½ cup carrots, grated
4 cups milk
2 tablespoons all purpose flour
1 teaspoon nutmeg
2 chicken stock cubes
1 teaspoon salt
3 teaspoons sugar

Batter:
1 cup all purpose flour
2 cups milk
2 eggs
pinch of salt
1 cup breadcrumbs
oil for frying

SAMBAL GORENG KERING KENTANG

FRIED POTATOES IN SPICY DRESSING

My Aunt Rora often made this as a side dish, but it is also very good just for snacking on. These crunchy fried matchsticks potatoes are doused with spicy seasoned dressing. They can be kept fresh by storing in an airtight container.

Heat the oil and sauté the onion, then add the garlic to fry lightly. Add the sambal oelek, diluted terasi, laos, salt and brown sugar, as well as the diluted asam or vinegar. Stir well to dissolve the sugar. Add the salam to warm through briefly. Remove from heat when the sauce begins to reduce and thicken. Add the potatoes and mix well to coat them all over with the sauce. Allow to cool before eating.

Tip: Toss a couple of handfuls of unsalted, roasted redskin peanuts in with the potatoes. Use regular potato chips if matchsticks are not available.

1 onion, minced
2 tablespoons oil
2 cloves garlic, crushed
1 tablespoon sambal oelek
1 teaspoon fresh terasi (fermented shrimp paste) diluted with 2 tablespoons hot water
½-inch piece laos (galanga), crushed to release the juices
½ teaspoon salt
3 ½ ounces brown sugar
1 tablespoon diluted asam (tamarind) OR vinegar
2 salam leaves (Indonesian bay leaves)
1 pound lightly salted shoestring potato fries, potato chip sticks, or potatoes cut into matchsticks

SEROENDENG

SEASONED SAUTÉED COCONUT

Seroendeng is spicy fried coconut flakes, made from sautéed, grated coconut, and is often used as a side dish to accompany rice.

Put the coconut into a wok, and mix it with the diluted terasi, diluted asam, garlic powder, ketumbar, djinten, laos, salam, djuruk purut, kentjur and 1 tablespoon of water. Cook over medium-high heat, stirring continuously. Add the oil when the mixture begins to look dry, continue toasting the coconut until golden brown. Add salt and sugar to taste, and add the peanuts at the end. Store in an airtight container in cool, dark place.

1 ½ pounds klapper (desiccated/ shredded unsweetened coconut)

1 teaspoons fresh terasi (fermented shrimp paste) diluted with 2 tablespoons hot water

1 small chunk asam (tamarind) diluted with 2 tablespoons hot water

¾ teaspoon garlic powder

4 teaspoons ketumbar (ground coriander)

1 teaspoon djinten (ground cumin)

½-inch piece laos (galanga)

2 salam leaves (Indonesian bay leaves)

4 djuruk purut leaves (kaffir lime leaves)

1-inch piece fresh kentjur (aromatic ginger / kaempferia galanga) OR ½ teaspoon ground kentjur

2 tablespoons oil

1 teaspoon salt

1 ½ tablespoons sugar

10 ounces roasted peanuts

KAASSTENGELS

CHEESE COOKIES

The Dutch word "kaas" means cheese and "stengel" means stalk. Some argue it should be spelled "tengels" which in Dutch means fingers. In any case, this savory cookie is finger licking good. This popular snack with Dutch roots has been adopted into Indonesian cuisine, where it is also known as "kastengel." In Holland we also see a longer variation made with puff pastry dough, twisted and then sprinkled with cheese before it is baked. They are traditionally served during the holidays, but nowadays enjoyed throughout the year. For the best cheese cookies use a Dutch mature cheese, such as aged Edam, aged Gouda or Old Amsterdam.

1 pound flour
½ pound butter, room temperature
3 egg yolks
½ pound mature cheese, grated
¼ teaspoon salt (or use salted butter)

Preheat the oven to 325° Fahrenheit. In a large bowl mix 2 egg yolks, butter, salt and cheese. Keep 4 tablespoons of cheese aside for on top. Add the flour to the mixture and stir to combine.

Turn the dough onto your work surface dusted with flour and knead a bit more. Separate the dough into mid size pieces and roll the pieces out to a thickness of ½ inch.

Brush the dough with beaten egg and sprinkle the top with grated cheese. Cut, to create small rectangular sticks, approximately 1" x 2" in size.

Bake in the oven until light brown (about 20 minutes). Keep in a cookie jar.

TIP: Use freshly grated Parmesan and mature cheddar as a substitute.

BITTERBAL & RUNDVLEESKROKET

DUTCH BEEF BALLS AND BEEF CROQUETTES

The bitterbal *and* kroket *are Holland's most popular meat-based snacks, containing a mixture of béchamel and minced or chopped beef or veal and spices. The* bitterbal *derives its name from a generic word for certain types of herb-flavored alcoholic beverages, called a* bitter *in Dutch, and are popularly served as part of a* bittergarnituur, *a selection of savory snacks to go with drinks, at pubs or at receptions in the Netherlands. This recipe makes about 10 kroketten or approximately 25 bitterballen (plural for kroket and bitterbal).*

Season the beef with salt. Heat butter in a skillet over medium heat. Cook onions until golden. Add the beef and cook for another 5 minutes. Add two cups of water and the stock cube. Bring to a boil and simmer for 2.5 hours on low heat until meat is tender. Remove the meat and chop finely. Set stock and meat aside.

Melt butter over low heat in skillet. Stir in the flour with a whisk to make a roux and the mixture comes together in a loose dough. Gradually mix in the stock and cook while stirring for about two to three minutes until done. Stir in the (squeezed/powder) gelatin. Add the egg yolk and the parsley. Add the meat to the mixture and bring to taste with pepper, salt and nutmeg. Pour the mixture into a square dish (approximately 9" x 9") and spread out evenly. Refrigerate overnight (or at least 2 hours) to stiffen.

Slice the mixture in 10 even rectangular pieces and shape each bar into a cylindrical kroket or make 25 evenly-cut squares and shape into balls by rolling each portion into your lightly oiled hands.

For the breading, put the flour, egg whites, and breadcrumbs in 3 different soup plates. One by one, cover the kroket or bitterbal with flour, egg white and then cover it all over with breadcrumbs. Deep-fry to a golden brown for about 4 minutes in oil of 355° Fahrenheit. OR: Heat oil to 355° Fahrenheit and deep-fry to a golden brown in about 4 minutes.

TIP: Serve the kroket on a slice of bread or hot dog bun.

14 ounces chuck roast, cubed
salt
2 ounces butter
2 cups water
1 stock cube
1 egg yolk
1 tablespoon chopped parsley
1 medium onion, finely chopped
6 tablespoons flour
4 gelatin sheets or 1 tablespoon powder
pepper
salt
1 teaspoon nutmeg

flour
4 egg whites, stirred
1 cup breadcrumbs
4 cups oil for deep-frying

PICKLES & SAMBALS

ATJAR KETIMOEN

SWEET-AND-SOUR CUCUMBER

Wash the cucumbers and slice them down the middle lengthwise. Remove the seeds by running a spoon along the soft channel inside and hollowing out the cucumber. Slice the cucumber into sections.

Boil the water with the vinegar and sugar. The flavor should be sweet-and-sour. Remove the pan from the heat and add the shallots, cucumber and lomboks. Add the salt. The vegetables should stay crunchy. Allow to cool. Keeps approximately 3 days in an airtight jar, if refrigerated.

2 large cucumbers
4 cups water
2 cups vinegar
4 tablespoons sugar
6 ounces shallots, quartered
3 red lomboks (large chili peppers), deseeded and sliced thinly on the diagonal
1 tablespoon salt

ATJAR TJAMPOER

MIXED VEGETABLE PICKLE

Atjar tjampur is one of the most well-known pickles. Tjampur means mixed. It is a flavorful, refreshing condiment which goes well with spicy food. Also suitable as a garnish with bread or alongside cold fish and meat dishes or salads.

Boil the vinegar with the water, jahe, kunjit, kemiri nuts, garlic and mustard. Add the sugar little by little, keep checking until it tastes somewhat sweet, then add the salt. When the vinegar comes to a boil, add the cabbage leaves and carrots. Finally add the bell pepper and cucumber. Simmer for 5 minutes. Remove from heat and allow to cool. Refrigerate for 1 to 2 hours before serving.

4 cups water
2 cups vinegar
1 inch piece jahe (ginger root)
1 teaspoon kunjit (ground turmeric)
3 kemiri nuts, ground
3 cloves garlic OR 1½ teaspoons garlic powder
½ tablespoon mustard
3 tablespoons sugar
1 tablespoon salt
8 cabbage leaves, shredded
8 carrots, julienned (cut matchstick-style)
1 red bell pepper, sliced diagonally
1 cucumber, sliced lengthwise, seed column removed

ASINAN

PICKLED VEGETABLES

Asin is the Indonesian word for salty. The vegetables are preserved by soaking them in salty water. Asinan is a distant cousin of the Korean condiment kimchi as they share similar ingredients like cabbage, cucumber and salt, however in kimchi the salting process takes longer. The Indonesian version includes bean sprouts, chili and terasi.

Bring the vinegar with sugar and salt to a boil. Add the cabbage, the cucumber and the bean sprouts as soon as the water boils. Turn off the heat. Mix everything well to combine. Allow to cool and refrigerate overnight.

Drain the vegetables retaining the vinegar sauce to use for the peanut dressing. Put vegetables in a bowl and set aside.

In a bowl, mix the peanut butter with 1 cup of vinegar mixture. Add sambal oelek and salt. Gradually add more vinegar while stirring. Keep tasting until the right consistency has been reached. Save the remaining vinegar mix in bottle in the fridge.

Arrange the lettuce leaves on a serving platter. Place the vegetables on top and pour the peanut sauce over the vegetables. Sprinkle the fried peanuts over the sauce and top the asinan off with krupuk, crumbled by hand.

2 cups vinegar
1 tablespoon sugar
1 teaspoon salt
4 cabbage leaves, cut into strips
½ cucumber, diced
3 ½ ounces bean sprouts
2 tablespoons peanut butter
1 tablespoon sambal oelek
salt
5 butter lettuce leaves
2 ounces fried peanuts
krupuk

SAMBAL TAOTJO

TAOTJO-FLAVORED SAMBAL

Heat the oil and sauté the lomboks with the onion and garlic for about 2 minutes. Add the taotjo, sambal oelek, jahe, sugar, a pinch of salt and the cream of coconut. Simmer over low heat until the cream of coconut has boiled down and blended with the rest of the ingredients. Taste and add sugar as needed.

4 red lomboks and 4 green lomboks (large chili peppers), sliced diagonally into slivers

1 onion, diced

2 cloves garlic, grated

1 tablespoon oil

2 tablespoons taotjo (fermented soybean paste, salty tasting, use the crushed Indonesian type)

2 slices jahe (ginger root), about ½ inch diameter

2 tablespoons sambal oelek

1 tablespoon sugar

salt

1 cup cream of coconut

SAMBAL TERASI

TERASI-FLAVORED SAMBAL

Crush the terasi with the lomboks, tjabe, sambal oelek and lemon juice, and add salt and sugar to taste. Ready to serve. If terasi bakar is not available, toast some fresh terasi in a dry pan over low heat.

1 teaspoon terasi bakar (toasted shrimp paste)
5 red lomboks (large chili peppers), deseeded and chopped roughly
1 tablespoon tjabe rawit (small chili pepper) stems removed
½ tablespoon sambal oelek
½ tablespoon lemon juice
½ teaspoon salt
½ teaspoon sugar

SAMBAL BADJAK

JAVANESE SAMBAL ("PIRATE SAMBAL")

This recipe yields a larger batch. Allow it to simmer a fairly long time, so that it can be kept longer.

Heat the oil and sauté the onion and crushed garlic until translucent. Add the crushed kemiri nuts, sereh, laos, salam and djeruk purut to the pan. When the mixture becomes fragrant, add the sambal oelek, diluted asam and terasi. Lastly, add the cream of coconut, and then salt and sugar to taste. First add the sugar, taste the sambal, then add the salt. Continue simmering over low heat, stirring regularly, until the oil rises to the top.

7 shallots, diced OR 2 small onions, diced
6 cloves garlic, crushed OR 3 teaspoons garlic powder
2 tablespoons oil
6 kemiri nuts, crushed
1 stalk sereh (lemongrass) (use the bottom 2 inches), crushed
1 piece laos (galanga, 1 inch thick, 1 knuckle-length), crushed
2 salam leaves (Indonesian bay leaves)
3 daun djeruk purut (kaffir lime leaves)
2 cups sambal oelek
1 small chunk asam (tamarind) diluted with 2 tablespoons hot water
2 teaspoons fresh terasi (fermented shrimp paste) diluted with 2 tablespoons hot water
½ cup cream of coconut
3 tablespoons sugar
½ teaspoon salt

SWEETS & BEVERAGES

KELEPON

COCONUT AND PALM SUGAR DUMPLINGS

Kelepon is one of my favorite sweet surprises. It is simple to make; in Singapore and Malaysia it is known as onde-onde. Inside these delicate, green balls rolled in coconut is deliciously sweet, melted palm sugar, which explodes in your mouth unexpectedly. These are best when eaten fresh.

Place the rice flour into a bowl and gradually add the water and the green pandan flavor extract, while kneading with your hand. Stop adding water when the dough forms a ball and no longer sticks to your hand.

Take a teaspoon of dough and roll into a ball. With your finger, press a small well into the center, and add about a teaspoon of palm sugar. Press closed and roll back into a ball.

Continue making balls and repeat with the rest of the dough and palm sugar.

Bring a pan of water to a boil. Carefully slide a few of the dumplings into the boiling water. Do not cook too many at once, otherwise the temperature of the water will lower and the dumplings could stick together.

The dumplings are ready when they float to the surface. Remove from the pan with a slotted spoon and allow to cool briefly. Combine the salt and grated coconut, and roll the dumplings in this mixture while they are still sticky and warm. Serve immediately and enjoy!

4 cups rice flour (ketan flour)
1 ½ cups tepid water
5 drops green pandan flavor extract
6 ounces gula jawa (Javanese palm sugar)
1 cup coconut, freshly grated
½ teaspoon salt

DADAR GOELOENG

COCONUT AND PALM SUGAR-FILLED PANDAN-CREPES

Aunt Rora made the very best dadar gulung. You can wake me up in the middle of the night for these dainty crepes, colored with green pandan and filled with a heavenly mixture of shredded coconut and gula jawa. They go well with a nice cup of tea.

Place the flour into a bowl, make a small well in the center and crack the egg into the well. Slowly begin incorporating the egg into the flour, adding the santan or water and green pandan extract little by little, until it forms a smooth, lump-free batter. Add a pinch of salt. Melt the butter in a skillet (about 6" in diameter) and make crepes; they should retain their light green color. Do not let them get too brown.

Prepare the filling: Place the gula jawa in a saucepan with the water and bring to a simmer over medium high heat until dissolved. Add the shredded coconut, pandan leaves and salt; keep stirring until the mixture is combined and the moisture has evaporated. Discard the pandan leaves and set the mixture aside.

To assemble: Spoon 2 tablespoon of filling onto a crepe, 1 inch from the edge and sides. Fold the sides in, and roll up like a small burrito. Repeat with the remaining crepes. Serve and see how fast they go!

2 cups all purpose flour
1 egg
12 ½ ounces santan (coconut milk) or water
1 tablespoon green pandan flavor extract
pinch of salt
2 tablespoons butter

For the filling:
5 ¼ ounces gula jawa (Javanese palm sugar)
½ cup water
2 cups shredded coconut (unsweetened)
2 pandan leaves
pinch of salt

KWEE MANGKOK

STEAMED CUPCAKES

This is the Indo Dutch version of a cupcake, made with rice flour and steamed. Children love these fun colored cupcakes; they are served at many festive occasions.

In a bowl, combine the rice flour, yeast, warm water, salt and 3 ½ ounces thick santan and mix to a thick batter. Add the melted gula jawa and the other 3 ½ ounces coconut cream and blend well. Add a few drops of pink food coloring OR green pandan flavor extract to the batter. Cover the bowl with a damp cloth and set aside to rise for approximately 25 minutes.

Pour the batter into a pre-warmed cupcake pan and place in a steamer for 15 to 25 minutes, leaving lid tightly closed. The kwee mangkoks are done when a thin skewer or toothpick is inserted into the center; if it comes out clean, it is ready. Remove from the steamer to cool. Sprinkle the shredded coconut over the cupcakes.

3 ⅓ cups rice flour
3 tablespoons yeast
3 ½ ounces warm water
1 teaspoon salt
7 ounces thick santan (coconut cream), divided
7 ounces gula jawa (Javanese palm sugar), melted
pink food coloring OR green pandan flavor extract
1 cup shredded coconut

KWEE LAPIS

TWO-COLOR TAPIOCA LAYER CAKE

The name of this sweet, porridge-like cake with alternating colors comes from kwee *meaning "cake and pastry" and* lapis *meaning layers. The cake batter is steamed instead of baked in the oven.*

In a saucepan, heat the santan and salt with the pandan leaves and bring to a simmer. Remove the pandan leaves and set aside to cool.

In a bowl, combine the tapioca flour, rice flour and sugar. Add the santan gradually until you have a smooth batter.

Divide the batter into thirds. Blend red food coloring into one third, green coloring into another third, and leave the last third uncolored. Lightly grease a medium loaf pan with the oil and pour a thin layer of one color batter, distributing evenly over the bottom. Steam for 3 minutes. When the top of first layer is dry, add a layer of the next color "lapis" batter, steaming for 5 minutes. Repeat adding layers of each batter and steaming for 5 minutes for each layer until all the batter has been used. Steam the cake for 30 additional minutes until cooked through. Remove from the steamer and cool before serving.

3 cups thick santan (coconut cream)
pinch of salt
2 pandan leaves
3 ½ ounces tapioca flour
1 cup rice flour
1 ½ cups sugar
red and green food coloring
light vegetable oil (e.g. canola, sunflower, etc.)

PANDAN CAKE
PANDAN-FLAVORED SPONGE CAKE

This delicate, green sponge cake is a variation on angel food or chiffon cake. I sometimes call it Hit and Miss Cake: if you are not careful, it can easily become bantat *cake - a cake which hasn't risen. However, if you're successful, it will melt in your mouth.*

Preheat the oven to 350° degrees Fahrenheit.

In a large saucepan, heat the coconut cream, salt and 1 tablespoon green pandan extract. When it comes to a boil, remove from heat. Beat the egg yolks until pale and fluffy; in a separate bowl, beat the egg whites until it just reaches stiff peak. Add to the coconut cream mixture the flour, sugar, baking ground, cornstarch, 1 tablespoon green pandan extract and a pinch of salt and mix to combine. Transfer the egg yolks and egg whites to the mixture and blend gently, until smooth and lump-free. Grease an angel food cake pan and pour the batter to just under the rim. Place in the center of the preheated oven and bake for 30 to 45 minutes, until the cake has risen. Check for doneness by piercing with a thin skewer or toothpick; if it comes out clean, it is ready. Remove from oven to cool for at least 10 minutes before inverting onto a plate to serve.

TIPS:

- Start with all ingredients at room temperature.
- The batter should be completely free of lumps; sift the flour before use. Adding a pinch of salt to the flour prevents clumping. Should the batter begin to separate, try placing it over a warm water bath (au bain marie) and stirring.
- Your bowls and utensils should be dry and grease-free; clean thoroughly with hot water before use.
- Do not beat the egg whites for too long, otherwise it will be more difficult to blend with the yolks and flour. The cake can collapse when there is too much air in the batter, as it will not be sturdy enough to pull itself up. The batter will have insufficient strength to rise and will sink during baking or shortly thereafter.
- Set the oven no higher than a medium temperature. A tear across the top of the cake can be caused by the oven being too hot. The crust is formed too quickly and the uncooked batter inside expands and seeks an exit through the weakest point.
- Remove the cake from the pan only after it has cooled completely.

½ cup thick santan (coconut cream)
pinch of salt
2 tablespoons green pandan flavor extract
8 eggs, separated into 8 yolks and 6 egg whites
1 ½ cups self-rising flour, sifted
¾ cup sugar
1 teaspoon baking powder
1 tablespoon cornstarch
butter

PISANG GORENG

FRIED BANANAS

Why is a banana curved ? If they were straight they would topple over. Ok, that's a lame Dutch joke. Why is pisang goreng so unbelievably scrumptious? Discuss with your dinner guests when you make this recipe and delight them with tender bananas enveloped in a crunchy, deep-fried crust made from a very special batter. Drizzle with melted Javanese palm sugar and dust with ground sugar and cinnamon. Equally satisfying as a sweet snack or dessert. Success guaranteed!

Combine the egg, flour, vanilla sugar [extract], salt and beer and blend to make a smooth, lump- free batter. The batter should not be too thin or too thick: begin with 3 tablespoons of beer and gradually add 1 or 2 tablespoons more.

Slice the bananas diagonally into 5-6 sections. Roll the sections in the beer batter and deep-fry in a generous amount of hot oil until golden brown.

In a small saucepan, melt the gula jawa with 1 tablespoon of water over low heat. Just before serving, drizzle the syrup over the bananas and dust with ground sugar and cinnamon.

Tip: Serve with a scoop of coconut ice cream and whipped cream.

1 egg
4 tablespoons self-rising flour
1 sachet vanilla sugar or ½ teaspoon vanilla extract
pinch of salt
4 or 5 tablespoons beer
2 bananas
1 ¾ ounces gula jawa (Javanese palm sugar)
oil for deep-frying
1 teaspoon ground sugar
1 teaspoon cinnamon

ROTI KOEKOES

STEAMED SWEET BREAD

This steamed (koekoes) bread (roti) makes a satisfying snack, but can also be part of a breakfast when spread with butter, and a cup of hot tea on the side. My friend Hanneke Olson-Monod de Froideville has fond memories of her mother Wilhelmina's Roti Koekoes.

Beat the egg whites until stiff. Gently fold in the egg yolks one by one. Add the sugar, lemon-lime soda and a pinch of salt, and beat for approximately 10 minutes with an electric mixer. Gradually add the flour and mix until smooth and even. Divide 1/3 of the batter into a bowl and add the food coloring or cocoa ground.

Line insert of a steamer with parchment paper all the way to the edge. Heat water in a steamer and bring to a boil. Reduce the heat slightly so that there is still plenty of steam. Wrap a linen tea-towel around the lid (to ensure no water falls on the bread while steaming). Pour 2/3 of the white batter in the insert of the steamer. Add 1/3 of colored batter and swirl with a spatula to create a marble effect. Let it steam for 40 minutes with the lid on so the steam does not escape. Check to see if the cake has risen and is done with a toothpick after the first 20 minutes.

Remove the bread from the steamer and allow to cool before slicing into wedges.

4 egg whites
8 egg yolks
2 cups sugar
2 cups lemon-lime soda (7Up/Sprite)
pinch of salt
3 ⅓ cups all purpose flour
½ teaspoon pink food coloring or 1 tablespoon cocoa powder

KLAPPERTAART

COCONUT CAKE

Born in the era of the Dutch East Indies and well known as a specialty of Menado, North Sulawesi. Klappertaart is the Dutch word for Coconut tart. A guaranteed hit when you bring to family or friends to have with morning coffee or for dessert.

Preheat the oven to 350° degrees Fahrenheit.

Soak the bread in the liquid from the canned young coconut meat, then squeeze out excess moisture. Beat together the eggs, sugar and vanilla sugar. Add the bread, coconut, milk and butter. Transfer to an ovenproof dish and bake in the preheated oven for 45 - 50 minutes.

If using flour instead of the bread, first combine this in a saucepan with the milk and vanilla and cook for a few minutes over medium heat, then add the coconut and butter.

3 ½ ounces bread or 5 tablespoons all purpose flour
1 can young coconut meat, strands cut into thirds (available at Asian and health food supermarkets)
4 eggs
3 ½ ounces sugar
1 envelope vanilla sugar or 1 vanilla bean
1 cup milk
1 ½ tablespoons butter

SPEKKOEK

The alternating brown and white layers of this symbolic cake represent the merging of two cultures to me. There is a range of stories about the creation of spekkoek, inspired by a Western cake and enhanced with spices from the Far East. It is thought that spekkoek harks back to colonial times, influenced by the Dutch, as a substitute for speculaas, a spiced shortbread cookie traditionally enjoyed during the end-of-year winter holiday celebrations in The Netherlands. The word 'speculaas' is said to have derived from 'spices,' originating from the Spice Islands (the Maluku Islands). Another theory about the origin of spekkoek is that it hails from Germany, where Baumkuchen, also a type of layer cake, is made. Where the word 'spekkoek' came from also has various theories. The alternating layers resemble spek (Dutch for bacon or pork fat), and when cut, the knife glides through the cake like butter. Because of all the layers, this luscious, spiced cake is somewhat labor intensive; my mother would be in the kitchen for most of the day to bake it. To make it last longer, I used to nibble on it slowly, peeling off layer after layer. Sometimes I would even get it in my lunchbox, sandwiched between two slices of bread.

OMA'S SPEKKOEK

GRANDMA'S THOUSAND-LAYER SPICE CAKE

My friend Terri (Hanhart) Stern loved to surprise her Pa, James Hanhart, with Spekkoek. When he could no longer eat butter, she modified her recipe so that he could continue enjoying spekkoek!

Preheat the broiler to 465° Fahrenheit.

Stir together the butter and sweetened condensed milk until smooth and creamy. Separate the eggs. Loosen the yolks with a whisk, then add the super fine granulated sugar and vanilla sugar (or vanilla extract). Beat until pale and foamy, then combine with the butter.

Whip the eggs until bright, stiff peaks form. Fold the egg whites carefully into the butter mixture. Stir the salt into the flour. Divide the batter into two equal portions. Combine all the spices in a bowl and stir into one half of the batter for the brown layer, ensuring there are no lumps or white streaks. Leave the other half of the batter white.

Grease a round, 8 inch spring form cake pan with butter, and lay a circle of baking parchment in the bottom. Spoon 2 to 3 tablespoons of white batter into the pan and spread out to the sides with the rounded side of a spoon to create a very thin layer of approximately ⅛ inch. Slide the cake pan under the pre-heated broiler 6 inches from the heat to set and bake for 90 seconds until lightly golden; check for doneness with a toothpick. Remove from broiler and spread a thin layer of the brown (spiced) batter over the cooked white layer, placing back under the broiler for another 90 seconds until set. Repeat this process, baking each alternating layer after layer, until the cake is built up, ending with a brown layer. Turn off the broiler and leave the cake in the oven for 10 minutes with the door open. Allow to cool before serving.

4 ½ sticks (1 pound 1 ½ ounces) butter
2 tablespoons sweetened condensed milk
20 eggs
1 ½ cups superfine granulated sugar
2 sachets vanilla sugar OR 1 teaspoon
    vanilla extract
1 ¼ cups all purpose flour, sieved
pinch of salt

spices for the brown layer:
4 rounded teaspoons ground anise seed
8 rounded teaspoons ground cinnamon
5 rounded teaspoons ground cloves
2 rounded teaspoons ground nutmeg
2 rounded teaspoons ground cardamom

STROOPWAFELS

DUTCH CARAMEL-FILLED WAFERS

Stroopwafels are becoming increasingly popular in the USA. This Dutch delight usually imported from Holland can be found in many grocery stores. Now you can make them fresh at home and host a stroopwafel baking party. I use an electric waffle iron that makes two waffles (available online as electric cookie iron waffler or pizzelle iron). Use a timer to not overcook the dough. This recipe was shared by my friends Charlotte & Ron Smit and makes about 66 stroopwafels.

In a bowl, dissolve the yeast and 2 ½ tablespoons sugar in warm water and set aside for about 1 hour. Combine the melted butter, cinnamon and 3 ½ tablespoons sugar in a separate bowl, add the eggs one by one and gradually add the flour. Add the yeast mixture and mix to make a stiff dough. Turn out onto a floured surface. Knead by hand and let the covered dough rise in a warm place for 45 minutes. Knead the dough again briefly and roll into balls of about 1 ounce a piece (weight). Cover the balls and set aside for about 15 minutes.

In a saucepan, and heat remaining 10 ½ ounces of sugar, butter, vanilla, ground cinnamon and the syrup over medium heat. Continue stirring until the syrup thickens. Quickly cool pan in a large bowl of ice water.

Preheat the waffle iron. Press a dough ball in the iron and cook until golden brown (approx. 1 minute or until the iron stops releasing steam). Carefully remove the waffle with a spatula or knife. Using a round cookie cutter ring, cut off the edges of the waffles and split in half horizontally while they are still warm. Spread the syrup on one of the insides and gently press the halves back together. Set aside to cool.

TIP: To soften the caramel filling, place the stroopwafel on top of your tea or coffee cup for a few minutes, or pop in the microwave for 6 seconds.

Dough:
½ cup water
1 package (¼ ounce) active dry yeast
2 ½ tablespoons sugar
2 sticks unsalted butter, melted
½ teaspoon ground cinnamon
3 ½ tablespoons sugar
2 eggs
1.33 lbs flour, sifted

Syrup:
⅔ stick unsalted butter, melted
10 ½ ounces brown sugar
½ teaspoon vanilla extract
1 teaspoon ground cinnamon
2 cups syrup (treacle molasses or
    Karo dark corn syrup)

PANNENKOEKEN

DUTCH PANCAKES

These Dutch delights are found in many pancake houses in Holland. The best are the homemade pannenkoeken. They are not crepes nor flap jacks, they are medium sized and not too thin nor too thick. I like mine crispy around the edges. My favorite anytime meal comes with toppings galore, from savory to sweet! You can combine the toppings to your heart's content.

In a large bowl, sift together the flour and salt. Add the eggs and 1 cup of milk and mix well with whisk or electric hand mixer. Gradually pour in the rest of the milk and mix until smooth (thickness of runny European-style yogurt). Place the batter in the refrigerator for 30 minutes.

Heat a non-stick skillet over medium heat. Grease it lightly with butter.

Pour a small amount (ladle-full) of batter onto the griddle and tip griddle to spread the batter around into a thin layer. Cook until top is dry, 1 to 2 minutes. Flip pancake with wide spatula and cook until browned on the other side, 1 to 2 minutes more. Roll pancake on a plate. If your first pancake breaks, the batter is too thin; add a little flour and try again. Repeat until all the batter is used. Keep the pancakes warm in the oven or on a covered plate resting over a pan with warm water.

If you are using bacon or mushrooms, put those in the pan first and then cover with a layer of batter. Flip until both sides are light brown.

1 cup all purpose flour
2 cups milk
2 eggs
1 pinch salt
butter, melted

Toppings:
Maple syrup
Ground sugar
Ground cinnamon
Apple, peeled and sliced
Raisins
Cheese, grated
Bacon, chopped
Mushrooms, sliced

OLIEBOLLEN

DUTCH DONUTS

A Dutch delicacy, literally translated "oil balls," are traditionally served on New Year's Eve. Nowadays, these deep fried pastries, often credited as the precursor to the American donut, can be enjoyed throughout the year. Usually filled with raisins and apple and dusted with ground sugar.

In a small bowl, mix the yeast, sugar and milk together and soak for 10 minutes. Slowly mix in eggs, vanilla. Sift in the flour and salt and mix thoroughly to a smooth batter. Stir in the raisins and apples. Cover the bowl with a damp dishtowel and allow to rise for at least 1 hour.

Heat the oil in a deep fryer or deep pan to 350° Fahrenheit. Use two tablespoons to shape the dough into balls, and drop them carefully into the hot oil. Fry and turn until golden brown on all sides. Remove with slotted spoon and drain on paper towel. Dust with ground sugar. Serve stacked in a pile and dust with more ground sugar. Eat them warm while the outside is still crispy and the inside is soft.

TIP: you should be able to fry 5 oliebollen at a time. If the oliebollen are uncooked on the inside, the temperature of the oil is either higher than 350° Fahrenheit or lower due to overcrowding of the pan. Store leftover oliebollen in an airtight container at room temperature – they will keep for about two days. Reheat in a preheated oven at 390° Fahrenheit.

1 tablespoon active dry yeast (2 packages = ½ ounce)
3 tablespoons sugar
3 ½ cups lukewarm milk
2 eggs, beaten
½ teaspoon vanilla extract
4 cups flour
1 teaspoon salt
2 cups raisins
3 Granny Smith apples, peeled, cored and finely chopped
8 cups oil for deep-frying
ground sugar

VLAFLIP

DUTCH CUSTARD

Vla is a classic Dutch toetje *(Dutch word for dessert pronounced TOO-tjuh). In English it is called custard, a dairy product made from fresh milk, eggs, vanilla and thickened by heat. My father used to make me* vlaflip *served in a tall glass, consisting of 3 layers: strawberry syrup at the bottom, a layer of vanilla custard in the middle and topped off with yogurt.*

Pour the milk into a saucepan and scrape out the seeds from the vanilla pod into the milk. Also add the pod to the milk. Bring slowly to a boil. Simmer for 10 minutes, and remove the vanilla pod. Combine sugar, cornstarch, egg yolks and salt in a bowl and mix to make a smooth paste. Add a tablespoon of warm milk to the paste while stirring. Add another tablespoon of milk and keep stirring. When the paste is fluid and warm enough, add it to the rest of the milk in the pan, while mixing with a whisk or a hand mixer on low speed. Heat slowly and continue to stir (also across the bottom and along the edges), until the vla has thickened. Remove from heat, stir a moment and then pour the vla in a bowl and cover with plastic foil to avoid a skin forming on the surface.

In a tall glass, pour ¼ cup syrup, followed by ½ cup vla, then ½ cup yogurt. Top with a dollop of whipped cream and a strawberry, serve and enjoy!

TIP: You can try other fruit syrups. Serve with a tall spoon.

4 cups of milk
1 whole vanilla bean OR 3
 teaspoons vanilla extract
¼ cup sugar
3 tablespoons cornstarch
2 egg yolks
1 pinch salt
strawberry syrup
European-style yogurt

ROZENSTROOP & SODA GEMBIRA

ROSE SYRUP AND ROSE MILK SODA

I grew up with this drink, like so many Indo Dutch people. My late aunt Rora in New York made her own rose syrup as she could not find any ready made in the stores. I can still hear her say: "Oh, that's easy to make!" This refreshing drink can be enjoyed throughout the year with water over ice or with sweetened condensed milk (stroop soesoe) or with added carbonated water (soda gembira).

4 cups water
16 ounces rose petals, unsprayed
1 lb sugar
6 tablespoons lemon juice
sweetened condensed milk
carbonated water (soda water)

Bring water to a boil, remove from heat and gradually stir in the rose petals. Set aside to cool, then refrigerate overnight. Strain the rose water and dissolve the sugar in a pan while stirring over medium heat. Bring to a boil and simmer for about 10 minutes. Add the lemon juice and add a couple of drops red coloring (if needed). Store the syrup in a glass bottle.

TO SERVE:
For rozenstroop: add ¼ cup syrup over ice and fill up the glass with 1 cup water. For soda gembira: 4 tablespoons condensed milk, 2 tablespoons rose syrup, crushed ice and fill up with soda water. Ahhh… Refreshing!

TJENDOL

DESSERT DRINK

A chilled coconut milk beverage with slivers of tjendol, *made of hun kwe flour (mung bean flour) and gula jawa (Javanese palm sugar). If you can find one, use a traditional* tjendol *sieve, which has large, round holes. My friend Ellen Stok says Tjendol is her favorite Indies drink – mmm good!*

Place the pandan leaves, white sugar and gula jawa into a saucepan with 1 cup of water and bring to a boil. Pour through a sieve, reserving the liquid, and set aside.

Measure the mung bean flour with a cup and add to a pan. Using the same cup, add 6 times the amount of water to the pan with the flour and mix well. Boil the flour and water mixture with the green food coloring; remove from heat when the mixture becomes slightly translucent.

Place the tjendol sieve (or an ordinary aluminum plate perforated with holes) over a bowl full of iced water. Pour the batter into the sieve and press it through the holes with a spatula: the batter will fall through the holes as slivers (tjendol) into the cold water. Transfer the tjendol slivers to a colander to drain.

In a measuring cup, combine the coconut milk with the same amount of cold water, and add the salt.

Serve the tjendol in glasses. Spoon 1 tablespoon of tjendol slivers into each glass, add crushed or shaved ice and 2 tablespoons of the gula jawa sauce. Fill the glass with the diluted coconut milk and serve with a dessert spoon. The coconut milk should be slightly salty, and the brown gula jawa sauce very sweet, for optimum contrasting flavors.

Tip: serve with thinly-sliced nangka (jackfruit) on top.

3 ½ ounces white sugar
7 ounces gula jawa (Javanese palm sugar)
2 pandan leaves, cut into large chunks
½ package hun kwe flour (mung bean flour)
1 teaspoon green food coloring
2 cans thin coconut milk
½ teaspoon salt

MENU SUGGESTIONS

MEALS ON THE GO & SPECIAL OCCASIONS

I grew up in the Sixties and Seventies among foodies, and we often went to southern Europe during the summer. My grandma had a house near the coast along the Costa Brava, Spain. Whenever we traveled abroad we were exposed to all kinds of food. My brother and I were often encouraged to try something new at least once. If we hesitated, my parents would often use the Dutch proverb: "What a farmer doesn't know, he won't eat!" Unworldly farmers we were not! On our way to our vacation destination we would often mock fellow Dutch tourists going in the same direction, stowing their caravans full with large sacks of potatoes, cheese and canned split pea soup. In all fairness, I must admit that our trunk had a bag of raw rice, terasi, chili peppers and various spices. Oh, and when there was room, an electric rice cooker. We did this, of course, to prepare a true Indo Dutch meal for our Spanish friends.

My dad specialized in European gourmet cooking. He would always bring back culinary souvenirs from our European trips and would serve a new specialty at home, which helped us relive the fun we had during our last vacation. My favorite was his beef stroganoff flambé. His love for Spain was also reflected in the kitchen: gambas al ajillo, paella and gazpacho. He would also make delicious Swiss cheese fondue and Italian pasta dishes and he loved to barbeque. He would often prepare a sampler plate for the neighbors.

My brother and I were taught well in how to prepare for a long road trip. Whenever the family went on a road trip, my brother and I sat in the back seat with a little Indo snack box nestled in between us, which contained, besides sandwiches, lemper, risolles and pasteitjes. Obviously a tjabe rawit or a jar of sambal badjak was included for the adults! Also sweet snacks: dadar goeloeng, kelepon, surabaya cake, spekkoek, kwee lapis and kwee mangkok. The thermos of coffee or iced tea went along.

When it came to making menu suggestions to our restaurant guests, my father would often sit at their table to discuss the specialties of the day or he would just say: "Leave it to me!" and would take back their menus. He knew exactly what his regular guests would like. Here are some suggestions for different occasions and meals of the day:

Selamatan— wedding, etc.

The selamatan is a communal feast we inherited from the people of Java, during which a ceremonial meal is served on the occasion of a wedding, birth, funeral, new house, etc. Typically, a dish like nasi oedoek (boiled rice with coconut milk) is served, or tumpeng with nasi koening (yellow rice colored with tumeric) molded into a cone shape on a tetampah (flat basket). It was usually accompanied by the following dishes: sambal goreng kering, ikan teri, omelette strips, sambal goreng telor, oerap oerap, ajam opor, seroendeng, ketimoen, satay ajam, kroepoek oedang, sayur lodeh, frikadel djagoeng, frikadel ketan... And a variety of other dishes.

The *rijsttafel* (rice table) as it was served in the restaurant, consisted of the following dishes: Nasi poetih, crackers, pickles, frikadel, seroendeng, gado-gado, sambal goreng telor, daging roedjak, babi koening, ajam opor, bebotok, sajoer lodeh, oblo oblo, sate babi/ajam and roedjak manis. Obviously, different combinations are possible and it can be as elaborate as you want. Depending on the time available, a rijsttafel can be simple or very elaborate. Making a rijsttafel can be quite labor intensive and requires the necessary preparation. Most side dishes, especially the meat and sauce, can be prepared a day in advance. This also has the advantage of allowing the flavors to develop and marry for the dish to taste even better. On the day you serve it, only the vegetables and rice need to be cooked. The prepared dish can be warmed up in the oven in a baking dish just before serving.

The single serving of a rijsttafel is called nasi rames; rice in the middle, surrounded by a variety of dishes: sambal goreng dishes (dry fried, spicy meat and/or vegetables), seroendeng, pickles and crackers, plus satay ajam or babi and a bowl of sajur lodeh. Since the nasi rames plate is prepared and pre-portioned in the kitchen, there is no free choice of side dishes and dining at the table can be significantly shorter.

Breakfast

As was common in the former Dutch East Indies, different cold cuts and spreads were served with bread, alongside nasi goreng; stir fried leftover rice from the previous day with leftover meat and vegetables. Also, bread with cheese and jam, or bread with peanut butter and sambal, and boeboer ajam. My favorite is an open sandwich with ham, cheese and fried egg (uitsmijter).

Christmas & New Year's Eve

At Christmas we had the most delicious dishes on the menu, like shrimp cocktail or a tasty Parma ham with melon as appetizer. For the main course a stuffed suckling pig, stuffed turkey or stuffed chicken called ajam kodok (meaning frog), served with asparagus, green beans, carrots, peas, peach and pear filled with cranberries compote, delicious gravy, and hashbrowns. A typical Indo Dutch dish was Bebek Sewar Sewir - acid black chicken or duck.

Potluck

A gathering whereby all guests bring a dish to share. This will relieve the host(ess) of having to cook an extensive rice table all alone. Best is to agree beforehand who brings what to avoid the same dishes. Popular in my family are the Indo hot pockets like risolles, pasteitjes or lemper. Suggested main courses are bami goreng, Indische macaronischotel, Indische Pastei Toetoep. My favorite sweets to share are pisang goreng, cake surabaya or pandan cake, dadar goeloeng and if I have time, spekkoek.

Vegetarian Dishes

Here are some suggestions: gado gado (replace kroepoek with emping), toemis sajoeran, sajoer lodeh, sambal goreng kentang, emping belindjoe, tahoe telor petis and rempejek katjang. Replace terasi (shrimp paste) with vegetarian stock cubes for flavoring.

Gluten Free

Many dishes are gluten-free due to the common use of tapioca, mung bean or rice flour in Indo Dutch cuisine. A savory snack is lemper (rice rolls). Some desserts are made with glutinous rice (the name refers to its stickiness, it does not contain gluten). Popular desserts are kelepon, kue lapis and tjendol.

What's for dinner?

1. Sambal goreng boontjes, kroepoek, sambal terasi served with steamed rice

2. Babi ketjap, atjar tjampoer served with steamed rice

3. Frikadel pan, cucumber sticks, served with steamed rice

4. Bebotok, sajoer lodeh, seroendeng served with steamed rice

5. Babi pangang, ora arek, atjar ketimoen served with steamed rice

6. Gado gado, sambal goreng boontjes, tempeh goreng, served with steamed rice

7. Oedang wotjap, toemisan sajoer served with steamed rice

8. Dadar kebertoe, atjar tjampoer served with steamed rice

9. Hutspot with slices of beef and gravy

10. Pea soup served over rice with sambal badjak and kroepoek

What to drink?

My grandma always liked to drink coffee (black over ice) or tea with her food. We often drink a glass of ice-cold beer or just ice water.

I also like wine with my dinner. For the exotic, hearty dishes with spices and strong flavors, the following wines are recommended: Rieslings that are "off-dry" are favorable to dishes with chili peppers. Also, try Gewürztraminer or a Pinot Gris.

The wine must be floral in aroma. The taste must, depending on the dishes, give enough weight to counterbalance the spicy nature of the food (a hint of sweetness). It should also have enough acids, so it becomes kind of a marriage with the dish. The wine should not overpower. A more robust wine is acceptable when eating a meat dish like rendang.

White or red?

White, because everyone says so. Alsace wines are a good match for example. White, because it is more floral and red because it is spicier. Red is permitted, slightly chilled. Watch out for red with tannins – that's bitter and does not go well with the stronger flavored dishes. Spicy dishes can best be paired with fruity wines.

Sarina's Inn
Specialized
Dutch & Indonesian Food

Cecelia Verkouteren, Owner

3036 Foothill Blvd.   La Crescenta, Calif.   Phone 248-4725

THANK YOU!

The recipes in this book are tied to personal stories. I would like to acknowledge the people who, consciously or not, have inspired and supported me, have given me their wisdom and their trust, and gave their friendship at different stages in my life.

First, thanks to my loving wife Petra, for her patience and extra space created to carry out my project. The house-turned-studio was a minefield of pots and pans and we survived! My mom Jessy Chevallier for her recipes for a good life and her contributions to this book; my dad Billy Keasberry for showing me how to be an entrepreneur and building valuable relationships; my brother and best buddy Duncan, sister-in-law Lucienne and niece Kimberly Keasberry. Oma Lieke Keasberry van Beekom, Oma Dee Delhaye, Tante Nessy and Oom Koen Fajakoen- Saleh, cousin Peter von Liebenstein, cousin Annette Sulilatu, cousin Tjandra Fajakoen Saleh, Marisol, Riet and my cousins James, Sandra and Esther Keasberry.

Also, I would like to thank my family and friends in the USA who have been involved over the years and who have impacted my life:

My admiration for my opa Jan Chevallier, who was a very artistic gentleman, respected for his strength, integrity and optimism. He taught me to have a sense of humor about myself and about everyday life, to keep things in perspective, and to always stay in touch with my inner child.

My second parents: Oom John and Tante Rora Laurens, longtime friends of the family, as far back as the 1940s in former Batavia. They were known as the jetsetters from Long Island, NY. Oom John was a fine gentleman and my role model; Tante Rora was an elegant and resourceful woman. I was inspired by Oom John's story of how he brought his family to the US to build a new life for his family in the 1950s, starting a new career as Engineer at PanAm. They would regularly fly to Amsterdam for a long weekend to reunite with

family and friends and get their Dutch food fix (drop, kroketten and mokkataart). And while they stayed over, they planted the seed when I was just 5 years old of nurturing my passion to pursue the American dream! So did their daughter Margaret Laurens. They never stopped encouraging and believing in me. It was a long journey and I eventually made it happen. I am eternally grateful!

Thanks for the memories, Tante Erie, aka Jeanne Abels-Van Dulken, for always making me feel at home. She was a classy, energetic, optimistic and charming woman, who you would not expect to also be the tomboy that she was. She was respected and admired by family and friends, known for her generosity and for always sticking up for the underdog. She would tell you the truth to your face. Her house was her castle and a sign at the door said: "Only enter with a happy heart!" She was the "hostess with the mostess"; no one left on an empty stomach or with empty hands!

I appreciate the times spent with Tante Ad and Oom Tonny, who owned an Indo Dutch restaurant, Sarina's Inn in La Crescenta, California. I remember the fun times with them and their kids, my cousins Gerry, Elly and Mike Verkouteren and family. A special thank you to Angie and Kurt for helping me when I first settled in the USA and to my cousin Margaret Keasberry for giving me a job at her design company. I would also like to acknowledge the Van Beekom, Pietersen and Gout families.

The production of this book was a huge adventure. The entire process, from raising the funds, to designing the concept, to making the final picture and text correction, was a memorable experience and a trip that I have not made all by myself. I am very grateful to those people who have contributed to the realization of this cookbook: praise to Nicki Dennis & Inez Hollander for their hard work with translating and editing. Thanks to the team at Mascot Books: Susan Roberts, Ricky Frame and Naren Aryal. Special thanks to those involved with endorsements and videos: Mischa Kuga, Michael Passage, Wendy Both, Chandan St. Clare, Samba Schutte, Rene Creutzburg, Tess Kartel, Jamie, Fanette and Terri Stern, Aldo Chacon, Carla Lekkerkerker, Hanneke Olson, Dr Jon Perlman, Maurice Juwono, Marco Farnararo, Eleonore Barkey-Passage, Judy and Travis Pike and Jack Profijt.

All the backers who helped raise the funds for this 1st print special edition, via the crowdfunding platform Kickstarter. In particular, those who picked the reward 'three of a kind' whereby their name will be mentioned in this list, in alphabetical order by first name:

Adrian Amsberry, Andreas van de Geijn, Antoine Cornelis Van Overeem, Colette Temmink, Cor Steenstra, Elizabeth Loth, Hans H. Keizer, HartmutEggert.com, Henney Neys & Gijs Axt, Jan Joosten, Jane Tomczyck, Jelle Westra, Jennifer Duong, Joyce Vodege, Kim & Jaime, Lola Newman, Louise Brough, Lucy & Hans Pustelnick, Marcelle Wiesen, Margaret Laurens, Maureen de Schepper, May Jacobs Feiteira, Nieta Blondeau, Otille Cools, Priscilla Kluge McMullen, Richard C. Ernst, Rodney Swearingen, Rosabel Goodman-Everard, Shelby, Shirleen Frailich, Sylvia & Martin Kast, Janice Sloma Pieters, Suzanne Lundberg-Wennekendonk, Tammy Silva, Vivian Lokhorst, Yvonne Verburgt.

My fellow board members and volunteers at The Indo Project for supporting the cause of preserving and promoting Indo Dutch food culture: Priscilla Kluge McMullen, Kareen Richard, Linda Kimbrough, Ingrid McCleary, Eric Morgan, Louise Brough, Jan Krancher and Willem ten Wolde.

Our dear cats Lola and Ari for their entertaining distractions and for waking me up every day at the crack of dawn, so I could get the maximum out of each work day, not because they were hungry.

Finally, to all gourmands and connoisseurs: thank you for your warm comments and enthusiasm for my first cookbook in English.

IN LOVING MEMORY

Backers of this project who picked this reward, wanted the following dear people mentioned and honored, in alphabetical order by first name:

Curly Jolly Elisabeth Rijnders-Monod de Froideville
Eric ten Cate
Frits and Corry de Bree
Herbert and Maria Pootjes
Nancy de Beukelaar
Oma A.A. Koppenol-van Wensveen
Oma C.W.J. Croes
Reginius Hugo van Beekom "Reny"
Simon & Frederika van Lommel
Alfred T. Dietrich

I asked my Oom John to write something for my cookbook when I first shared my plan with him back in 2004. Here is an excerpt:

"The family and the restaurant were for me personally an important part of my life and still are. They were the topic of discussion in all three countries: Indonesia, the Netherlands and America. In 1953, Moes (aka Oma Keasberry) had the restaurant officially opened by the former mayor of Amsterdam, Mr. A.J. d'Ailly, as guest of honor. After some time, all 4-star hotels in Amsterdam recommended this restaurant to their guests for being an exotic, authentic piece of the Dutch East Indies and Indonesian culinary excellence, run by a family with roots in Djokja, Central Java, where these Keasberrys originally came from. Guests were treated to a superb gourmet meal and atmosphere. Always 'gezellig' and top notch. Thanks to three generations of extraordinarily dedicated people who have brought us this gift. We wish Jeffrey much success with the publication of this life's work in print."

John Laurens
New York - home of those who 'made it'
Nov 2004

GLOSSARY OF TERMS

Throughout this book I use different terms/adjectives. To better understand why and how they are used, please read the following explanations:

INDISCH (DUTCH WORD) OR INDIES refers to the former Dutch colony in Southeast Asia (not India), or frequently as a political concept and geographical indication of the area under Dutch control (that became Indonesia after World War II). Socio-culturally, it refers to the blended culture (subculture) made up of people that associated themselves with and experienced the colonial culture of the former Dutch East Indies. The Dutch Indies people can be roughly divided into two groups: Totoks and Indo-Europeans.

TOTOKS is an Indonesian language term colloquially used in Indonesia to refer to individuals of exclusive Dutch and other European ancestry who lived in the Dutch East Indies until Indonesian independence after World War II. A term popularized in the eighteenth and nineteenth centuries among colonists, initially coined to describe the foreign born and new immigrants of "pure blood" and later those that were born in the East Indies of exclusive European ancestry - not mixed with indigenous Asian people.

INDO-EUROPEAN(S) also abbreviated as INDO(S), are people acknowledged to be of mixed European and indigenous descent living in the Dutch indies. A mix of predominantly Dutch, and also Portuguese, British, French, Belgian, German and others with Javanese, Sumatran, Manadonese, Timorese, Amboinese, Chinese, Balinese, etc. The word Indo-European has been used since the nineteenth century during the height of Dutch colonial rule. The front part, Indo, is derived from the Greek *Indoi* which means India and in turn is derived from Indus. Indo in this context is not derived from Indonesia, which is a term coined by James Richardson in 1850 and used since 1900 in academic circles outside the Netherlands, and by Indonesian nationalist groups. During that time the term Indo-European was already used

in literature. During Dutch rule the Indos (short for Indo-Europeans) were considered Europeans possessing the Dutch nationality. Despite this, the Indo considered himself as different from the 'imported Dutch', also known as 'totok'. The reason for this is their mixed ancestry. Throughout the years, the Indos developed their own hybrid culture, a combination of oriental and European (Dutch) customs.

INDO DUTCH is the preferred English term used most in my book when referring to the people of mixed race and the subculture. The first part of the word refers to the mixed Indo-European subculture and Dutch refers to citizenship. The Indonesian term is 'Indo Belanda.' In the English language the term Dutch-Indonesian is often used. I believe that to be incorrect, as the people I refer to were not Indonesians. In my case I have Indo-European heritage and was born and raised in the Netherlands and have Dutch citizenship. With Indos there will always be the link between Indonesia and Holland. In the Dutch language the term Indische Nederlanders (Dutch Indies people, which is more inclusive) was often used in the sense of 'being of Western culture,' which was the case in the colonial period.

When I talk about Indo Dutch cuisine, I mean the cooking style and food culture that originated in the former Dutch East Indies centuries ago, which evolved and was brought with the Indo Dutch (Indo Europeans - Indischen) people to migratory countries. Adopted dishes from Indonesia, Holland and a fusion of both coming together in one unique cuisine. The cooking style left marks in the national cuisines and influenced food customs of both countries.

For the names of ingredients I have chosen the modern spelling and how it is known in the English language. For the names of dishes I have opted to stay faithful to the old Indo Dutch spelling. When you see 'oe' that is the old spelling for 'u' and is pronounced as 'ooo' in 'boo'. Sometimes you will see 'c' or 'tj' in names, which is pronounced as 'ch' in 'check'.

A

Agar-agar jelly or a binder prepared from
      seaweed
Ajam chicken
Asam tamarind, acid
Asam garem tamarind and salt
Asin salt, salted
Atjar pickles
Atjar tjampoer chopped mixed pickles

B

Babi pig, pork
Bajem kind of nettle, spinach
Bakar burning, dry baking, roasting
Bami Chinese noodles
Basah wet, moist
Bawang onions, leeks
Bawang merah red onion, shallot
Bawang poetih garlic
Bébék duck
Belimbing starfruit
Beras raw rice
Blado with peppers
Boeboer porridge mash or puree
Boemboe Javanese herbs, spices
Boentoet tail
Botol bottle
Brambang red onions
Bras or beras uncooked peeled raw rice

D

Dadar omelet, egg contents
Daging meat
Daoen leaf
Dapoer kitchen, oven
Dendeng dried, seasoned thinly sliced meat
Djagoeng corn
Djamoe herb
Djeroek citrus, lemon

Djeroek nipis type/variety of small lemon
Djinten or djintan cumin
Dodol sweet delicacy of glutinous rice

E

Ebbi dried shrimps
Empal meat dish
Emping belindjoe vegetable crackers
      (melindjo)
Es ice

F

Frikadel minced meat, meatloaf

G

Garam or garem salt, table salt
Goela djawa Javanese palm sugar
Goerih spicy, tasty, tasty savory
Goreng fried in oil, roast
Gosong burnt

I

Idjo green
Ikan fish
Ikan asin salted fish
Ikan kering dried fish
Ikan pindang salted, dried, pickled fish
Ikan teri anchovy-like fish (dried / salted)
Isi filling, stuffing, content

J

Jahe ginger

K

Kajoe manis kaneel
Kambing goat

Kangkoeng ferrous marsh plant
Kapulaga cardemom
Kari curry
Katie Indonesian pound (617 grams)
Katjang bean, pea, legume
Kelapa coconut
Kelapa Moeda young coconut
Kembang flower
Kemiri type of nut
Kenarie type of almond
Kentang potato
Kentel thick (moisture), syrupy
Kentjoer Kaempferia galanga rhizome or
      galanga kaempferia
Kepiting crab, lobster
Kering dried
Ketan glutinous rice (white or black)
Ketella pokong cassava
Ketimoen cucumber
Ketjap soy sauce
Ketjap asin light sweet soy sauce
Ketjap manis sweet soy sauce
Ketoembar coriander
Ketoepat rice in woven baskets
Klapper coconut
Kloewek type/variety of nut/kernel of the
      fruit timboel
Koekoesan braided rice steamer
Koening yellow
Koenjit, koenjir turmeric
Koerang deficiency, less
Koetjai chives, leeks
Koewah, kuah sauce or wet dish
Kopi coffee
Kretjek crispy fried strips of buffalo skin
Kring, kering dry
Kripik fried slices ketella chips
Kroepoek oedang shrimp cracker as a
      condiment with rice
Kwee, kwé biscuit, cake

L

Lada pepper
Laksa Chinese vermicelli (su-un)
Lalap cold vegetable dish, raw
Laos rhizome of Alpinia galanga
Lapis from Dutch word lapjes, layering
Lemper rolls of sticky rice with chicken or
    meat filling
Limau lemon
Liwet boiling in a pot, not steamed
Lombok big chilies
Lombok merah large red chilies
Lombok rawit hot small chili
Lontong compressed rice in bags

M

Makan food (verb)
Mampir swinging by people's home
    (family, friends or neighbors)
Mangkok cup, bowl
Manis sweet
Mata sapi literally cow's eye, fried egg
Mie Chinese noodles
Mihoen Chinese vermicelli from rice flour
Moeda young

N

Nangka jackfruit
Nasi cooked rice
Nasi goreng fried rice

O

Oebi sweet potato, root vegetable
Oedang shrimp
Oelek mash, pounded
Oelekan pestle
Oerap oerap mix, mixed vegetable dish

P

Padi rice
Pala nutmeg
Panas hot, warm, excited
Pangang roasted
Pasar maket
Pedis tart flavor, spicy, hot
Perkedël frikadel
Peteh stink bean
Petis oedang shrimp paste
Pisang banana
Pisang radja small kind of banana
Pisang tandoek type of banana used for
    baking
Poetih white

R

Ramboetan fruit with hairy skin
Reboeng young bamboo shoot
Rendang spicy meat dish
Roedjak fruit salad with seasoned soy
    sauce
Roti bread

S

Sajoeran vegetables
Salam leaf
Sambal mashed lombok
Santan Kental thick coconut milk, 1st
    pressing
Santan coconut milk
Santan entjer thin coconut milk
Santan kentel thick coconut milk
Sapi cow, beef
Selamat (slamat) makan enjoy your meal
Selasi basil
Selassie seeds for cool drinks
Sereh lemon grass
Seroendeng sautéed grated coconut with
    peanuts

Singkong cassava, see ketella
Soesoe milk
Sop soup

T

Taotjo fermented soybean paste
    (Japanese miso)
Tahoe curd made from mashed soybeans
Tampah tetampah flat basket
Tanggok spherical sieve
Taotjo Java sugar and soybeans
Tapioca starch from cassava plant
Taugé sprouted soybean
Telor egg
Telor asin salted egg
Temoekoentji type of root
Temoelawak type of root
Tempeh cake of fermented soybeans
Tepung flour
Tepung beras rice flour
Teri small anchovies
Terong eggplant
Tim cooking or stew in a pot
Timoen tikoes pickle
Tjabe kind of chili pepper
Tjampoer mixing
Tjampoeradoek mixed sour vegetables
Tjendol refreshing drink with coconut milk
    and palm sugar
Tjengkeh cloves
Tjeplok fried egg sunny side up
Tjobek mortar
Toemis sautéed vegetables
Toetoep closed
Trassi or terasi fermented shrimp paste
Trassi bakar roasted shrimp paste

W

Wadjan Indonesian wok with two handles

RECIPES OVERVIEW

INDEX OF DISHES

IN ALPHABETICAL ORDER BY ENGLISH DESCRIPTION

RESOURCES

PHOTOGRAPHS CREDIT

Food styling by Jeff Keasberry

Food pictures by Jeff Keasberry, except for:

Nationaal Museum van Wereldculturen. Object number TM-60011222 Cornelis de Houtman Java – page 14 & 15

Rijsttafel Bandoeng TM-10030167 – page 34

De Soos Pasadena – Nicola Draculic – page 27

Shutterstock pages 24 & 25, 46 & 47, 52 & 53, 68 & 69, 132, 170 & 171

Erick Kyogoku – page 202 & 203

Daniel Gundlach – page 10

Eddie Vita: pages 28, 83, 95, 99, 114, 124, 129, 136, 175, 178, 181, 187, 211, 213

Duncan Keasberry – page 216

Armando Ello - page 75, 207

RESOURCES RECOMMENDED SPECIALTY STORES

VANDER VEEN'S DUTCH STORE, 2755 28th St SW, Grand Rapids, MI 49519, www.TheDutchStore.com

THE LITTLE DUTCH GIRL, 210 Gentry Street, Spring, Texas 77373. www.littledutchgirl.com

HOLLAND INTERNATIONAL MARKET, 9835 Belmont St. Bellflower, CA 90706 www.hollandintmarket.com.

WWW.KEASBERRY.COM

RESOURCES USED AS REFERENCES IN THIS BOOK

Met kruiden en een korrel zout, Derksen, Ellen, Tong Tong, Den Haag 1994

Indisch ABC – Hans Jacobs en Jan Roelands, Amsterdam – Uitgeverij De Arbeidspers-MCMLXX NedIndie.nl – Bert van der Velden

Indisch Informatiepunt – Rick van der Broeke

The Genealogy of the Keasberry family (keasberry.net) - Lodewijk Egbert Keasberry

"Ajoh dan, neem… neem – De Geschiedenis van de Rijsttafel' – Joop van de Berg 's-Gravenhage 2002

NCRV 1976 Dik Bikker – Transcript Radio Interview program with Oma Keasberry: de zomer van toen, de zomer van 1950.

Exhibit on 'Geschiedenis Indische Keuken (History Dutch Indies Cuisine) – Stichting Tong Tong Fair – The Hague 2011 – 2013

WEIGHTS & MEASUREMENTS

MEASUREMENT CONVERSIONS

All measures of spoons are level unless otherwise stated.

Standard spoon and cup measurements used are 1 cup = 250ml.

1 tablespoon = 15 ml 1 teaspoon = 5ml.

For the following ingredients comparable measurements apply:

Sereh: 1 stalk = 1 teaspoon powder

Chili Pepper: 2 fresh = 1 level tablespoon sambal oelek

Garlic: 2 cloves = 1 level tablespoon powder

Ketumbar & Djinten to be used in the ratio 2:1.

	VOLUME		LIQUID	
U.S.	METRIC	IMPERIAL	METRIC	IMPERIAL
1 TEASPOON	5 ML	⅙ FL OZ	15 G	½ OZ
1 DESSERTSPOON	10 ML	⅓ FL OZ	30 G	1 OZ
1 TABLESPOON	15 ML	½ FL OZ	55 G	2 OZ
2 TABLESPOONS	30 ML	1 FL OZ	60 G	2 OZ
¼ CUP / 4 TBSP	60 ML	2 FL OZ	70 G	2 ½ OZ
⅓ CUP	85 ML	2 ½ FL OZ	85 G	3 OZ
⅜ CUP	90 ML	3 FL OZ	110 G	4 OZ
½ CUP	125 ML	4 FL OZ	150 G	¼ LB
¾ CUP	180 ML	6 FL OZ	225 G	⅓ LB
1 CUP	250 ML	8 FL OZ	350 G	¾ LB
1 ¼ CUP	300 ML	10 FL OZ (½ PINT)	450 G	1 LB
1 ½ CUP	375 ML	12 FL OZ	500 G	1 LB, 1 ½ OZ
1 ¾ CUP	435 ML	14 FL OZ	700 G	1 ½ LBS
2 CUPS	500 ML	16 FL OZ	800 G	1 ¾ LBS
2 ½ CUPS	625 ML	20 FL OZ (1 PINT)	1 KILO	2 LBS, 3 OZ
3 CUPS	750 ML	24 FL OZ	(1 ⅕ PINTS) 1.5 KILOS	3 LBS, 4 ½ OZ
4 CUPS	1 LITRE	32 FL OZ (1 ⅗ PINTS)	2 KILOS	4 LBS, 6 OZ
5 CUPS	1.25 ML	40 FL OZ (2 PINTS)		
6 CUPS	1.5 LITRES	48 FL OZ (2 ⅖ PINTS)		
10 CUPS	2.5 LITRES	80 FL OZ (4 PINTS)		

TEMPERATURE	
°C / GAS MARK	°F
120/1/2	250
135/1	275
150/2	300
160/3	325
180/4	350
190/5	375
200/6	400
220/7	425
230/8	450
245/9	475
260	500

LENGTH	
INCH	METRIC
1/4 INCH	0.5 CM
1/2 INCH	1 CM
3/4 INCH	1.5 CM
1 INCH	2.5 CM
6 INCHES (1/2 FT.)	15 CM
12 INCHES (1 FT.)	30 CM